the
way
of
transition

Other Books by William Bridges

Transitions:
Making Sense of Life's Changes

Managing Transitions:
Making the Most of Change

JobShift:
How to Prosper in a Workplace Without Jobs

Creating You & Co.:
Learn to Think Like the CEO of Your Own Career

Surviving Corporate Transition:
Rational Management in a World of Mergers,
Layoffs, Start-Ups, Takeovers, Divestitures,
Deregulation, and New Technologies

The Character of Organizations:
Using Jungian Type in Organizational Development

A Year in the Life

the
way
of
transition

embracing life's most difficult moments

WILLIAM BRIDGES

PERSEUS PUBLISHING
Cambridge, Massachusetts

A Catalog Card Number for this book is available from the Library of Congress.

ISBN 0-7382-0410-2

Perseus Publishing is a member of the Perseus Books Group

Text design by Jeff Williams
Set in 10.5 Minion by Perseus Publishing Services
First printing, December 2000
  2 3 4 5 6 7 8 9 10—05 04 03 02 01

Perseus Publishing books are available at special discounts for bulk purchases in the U.S. by corporations, institutions, and other organizations. For more information, please contact the Special Markets Department at HarperCollins Publishers, 10 East 53rd Street, New York, NY 10022, or call 1–212–207–7528.

Visit us on the World Wide Web at http://www.perseuspublishing.com

To Susan. . . and a new beginning

contents

acknowledgments

With special thanks to Jim Trupin and Liz Trupin-Pulli, who kept on with the project when publishers were discouraging. To Susan Williams who made me believe in it when I was losing hope. And to Marnie Cochran who helped me bring it home.

prologue

No story is the same to us after a lapse of time; or
rather we who read it are no longer the same
interpreters.

George Eliot

Life has a way of bringing you back to places that you thought that you had left for good. I had begun my second career in 1980—my first was teaching American literature—with a book on personal transition. That had led me into work with organizations, since it was often their mergers, reorganizations, and technological changes that put people into transition. Organizational transition led me even further beyond personal transition, and I started writing about the disappearance of traditional jobs from today's workplace. With the publication of *JobShift* in 1994, I believed that I had left the topic of personal transition behind me.

But less than a year later, I found my life plunged into chaos. Mondi, my wife of thirty-five years, discovered a small lump in her left breast, and we began a long struggle with cancer. For the next two years, we rode a roller-coaster of hope and disappointment. Although she had enough good times so that we sometimes believed that the cancer was gone, it kept coming back. Finally, in May 1997, only a month after she had been enjoying a particularly good remission that we imagined might mean recovery, she died.

For several months after her death, I didn't do any speaking and training on the subject of transition. At first, I simply lacked the energy for any sort of activity—least of all one that required me to inform and entertain an audience. But I found that, as glad I was for the chance to rest, I also missed the structure and purpose that work had always given to my life, the chance it provided me to be out around people, and the feeling it gave me of being productive.

After three months of inactivity, I tried a few small projects and found that being busy again felt good. But working also presented me with an unforeseen new problem. All the things that I had written about transition—the very things that people had said were so helpful to them—now felt strangely unreal to me. I wondered, *How could I ever have tried to pass myself off as an expert on transition?* I felt now that my words had totally failed to match in depth the *experience* of actually being in transition.

I began to have a troubling fantasy: that during all those years, people who were in transition had come to my speeches and picked up my books looking for help and had gone away hungry. Worse, I imagined that they had resented my belief that I had something to say. This feeling became so strong that I decided to stop speaking or writing on the subject completely for a while, though even that decision didn't save me from the shame of having talked so long about something I now doubted that I knew anything about.

I felt as if my whole career as an expert on transition had been a fantasy out of which I had been pulled by a jolt of reality. I could not imagine ever speaking or writing on the subject again. That frightened me, because if I stopped doing that work, I would lose not only my livelihood but also one of the important continuities in my life. It wasn't that I was tired of thinking about the topic of transition. Quite the opposite: nothing was more interesting to me than it was now. It was just that I couldn't imagine how to say anything that would match the depth of the experience I was having.

It took me some time to realize that these feelings were an expression of the *disenchantment* that I had always said was part of the transition experience. If it is deep and far-reaching, transition makes a person feel that not only is a piece of reality gone, but that everything that had seemed to be reality was simply an enchantment. With the spell broken, life can look so different that we hardly recognize it.

Gradually I decided that whenever an old reality disappears, the answer is not to refuse to do anything that had been associated with it, but rather to explore and discover what the new reality is. What did my own huge encounter with transition tell me? What would I say now if I were to speak about the subject for the first time?

Those were difficult questions, both because they forced me to rethink everything I had thought that I knew and because they threatened to bring a perfectly good career and reputation for expertise crashing down around me. Who am I, I wondered, if I no longer possess that expertise? Ah, yes, I thought. I know what is going on. Transition doesn't simply disenchant: it breaks up your old identity too. I had talked about that aspect of transition as well, calling it *disidentification*, and people had thanked me for my insight.

I had also talked about *disorientation*. And I did indeed feel disoriented. . . lost. . . didn't know which end was up. Maybe I *had* known what I was talking about all those years. Maybe it was just that the subjective experience was far more poignant than verbal descriptions can convey. Deciding that made me feel a little better.

I was fortunate to be able to take some time off from work after Mondi died in the spring. The break gave me a chance to get a little more familiar with my new reality. By late summer, I was trying a few speeches, and in the early fall I took a business trip to Europe during which I made several more speeches. I had moments of self-doubt when I half expected someone to get up and denounce me as a charlatan, but I found myself saying some new things that I didn't know that I knew.

On that trip, I also took a few days by myself in Wales, driving a tiny Fiat down narrow roads and walking to the sites of ruined abbeys in deserted valleys. Although at home I lived alone now, this was a different kind of aloneness. Now I could appreciate first-hand why people in transition have so frequently gone on pilgrimages. I even went out of my way to find sites reputed to be specially sacred ones. Was it my imagination, or did I really feel a newly powerful spiritual presence as I sat beside a sacred well or walked up the aisle (now carpeted with grass) of a long-abandoned monastery that had once been the destination of pilgrims? In this new and different landscape I experienced myself afresh and came to see how personal transition can open up vistas that are rightly called *spiritual*.

An idea began to take shape, although it was several months before I could fully articulate it. The disorientation that I was experiencing (like the disidentification and disenchantment that created it) was beginning to feel not like a terminal state but like a prelude to something new. The ending that had taken place and the loss that I had experienced were, I started to feel, the psychic ground-clearing operation that might make new building possible. This new experience of being in transition might give me a new understanding of transition and new ways of helping people to find meaning in it.

William Wordsworth said that art is passion "recollected in tranquillity." I don't believe that I have reached the tranquil part of the experience yet. But I no longer feel overwhelmed by my transition. I can reflect on it, hold it at arm's length and consider anew what transition really is and what it does to a person. I can speak both as someone who has worked with people in transition for twenty-five years and also as someone who has gone through a big one recently.

In writing this book, I want to keep my perspectives straight and to do justice to both points of view—the conceptual and the experiential. Toward that end, I have clustered my ideas and my personal story into different chapters and moved back and forth between these two different perspectives on transition. I have a feeling that truth—whatever that battered word means—can only come from such binocular vision.

My earlier work on transition came out of my forties and fifties. It still seems valid to me, but the world and I have changed. What follows is how transition looks and feels to me—now, today, at sixty-six, at the beginning of the twenty-first century, at this cross-roads in my life. At this time of endings-and-beginnings. Out of this strange emptiness that I call the neutral zone. As I emerge from my own transition.

Mill Valley, California
July 2000

one

Change and Transition

There is no sin punished more implacably by nature
than the sin of resistance to change.

Anne Morrow Lindbergh

It's a paradox: To achieve continuity, we have to be willing to change. Change is, in fact, the only way to protect whatever exists, for without continuous readjustment the present cannot continue. Even the great conservative, Edmund Burke, realized this, for he said that "a state without the means of some change is without the means of its continuation."[1] The refusal to change will not guarantee that whatever we care about stays the same. It only assures that whatever we care about has been deprived of the very thing it needs in order to survive. A marriage, a career, a dream for the future, even a picture of the past: Each of these things is being primed for destruction if it does not change over time.

Here is another paradox: The very things we now wish that we could hold onto and keep safe from change were themselves originally produced by changes. And many of those changes, in their day, looked just as daunting as any in the present do. No matter how solid and comfortable and necessary the *status quo* feels today, it was once new, untried and uncomfortable. Change is not only the path ahead, but it is also the path behind us, the one which we traveled along to wherever we are now trying to stay.

But in spite of being necessary, most people would tell you that change is something that we "naturally" resist. If you ask them to account for that resistance, they talk about how we fear the unknown so much that we stick with even uncomfortable situations rather than venture into unfamiliar territory. Or they talk about how our natural selfishness makes us refuse to give up whatever we have or how most people's limited outlook hides other possibilities from them. They may talk about how "inflexible" most our personalities are.

Having worked with both individuals and organizations on transition-related problems for twenty-five years, I would say that most people *do not* resist change. What we resist is transition. "Transition" and "change" are words that are often used as though they were synonymous, but they really aren't.

Change is a situational shift:

- Getting a new boss is a *change*, and so is receiving a promotion or losing your job;
- Moving to a different house is a *change*, and so is remodeling your house or losing it in a fire;
- Having a new child is a *change* for everyone in the family— including the new baby, who was pretty well situated before all the change took place;
- And, of course, losing a loved one is a *change*—a huge one.

Transition, on the other hand, is the process of letting go of the way things used to be and then taking hold of the way they subsequently become. In between the letting go and the taking hold again, there is a chaotic but potentially creative "neutral zone" when things aren't the old way, but aren't really a new way yet either. This three-phase process—ending, neutral zone, beginning again—is transition.

Transition is the way that we all come to terms with change. Without transition, a change is mechanical, superficial, empty. If transition does not occur or if it is begun but aborted, people end up (mentally and emotionally) back where they started, and the change doesn't work. In spite of the new boss (or the new house or the new baby), nothing is really different.

When we resist transition, we resist one or more of the three phases of its makeup. We may resist *letting go* of the old; we may resist the confusion of the in-between *neutral zone* state; or we may resist the uncertainties of making a risky new *beginning*. We resist transition not because we can't accept the change, but because we can't accept letting go of that piece of ourselves that we have to give up when and because the situation has changed.

We also resist transition because it takes longer (often much longer) than change, and so it leaves us in limbo—or in *the neutral zone*, as I prefer to call it—while a replacement reality and a new self is gradually being formed. Although the change itself may immediately go straight from old to new—you live in one house one day and in another the next—transition always makes us spend a surprising amount of time in that uncomfortable in-between neutral zone. It is a long while after we arrive in the new house before we begin to feel at home there. And looking back, we realize that we felt as though we were in transition during those last weeks in the old house, too. Even the prospect of a change can put us into transition.

Another reason that people resist transition is that it sets up "resonance" between the present and painful experiences in the past. It is as though the later experience of loss "vibrates" and sets other, older losses on the same wavelength, vibrating sympathetically. A person who lost a parent during childhood, for example, is likely to be especially vulnerable to the ending of an adult relationship, as well. People whose lives came apart once because of a difficult physical move that took them away from everyone they cared about, are likely to find subsequent moves upsetting. And people with childhood experiences of profound failure—the kind that leave you feeling worthless and hopeless—can be especially vulnerable to experiences in which their sense of personal worth or adequacy is challenged.

In removing the status quo, transition not only recalls old hurts, it also threatens to throw us back into the state we were in before the status quo was established. The circumstances of our adult lives (the homes we live in, the friends we have, the work we do, the families we are part of) often serve to protect us from painful recollections of the way we used to feel about ourselves before those things existed. When those circumstances go away or fall apart, we are left exposed to our old self-doubts and anxieties. It is no accident that it is the pain triggered off by transition that often leads people into psychotherapy, or that one of the tasks they face in psychotherapy is to disentangle present realities (which may be painful enough in their own right) from the remembered traumas of the past.

• • •

It is not the conscious changes made in their lives by men and women—a new job, a new town, a divorce—which really shape them, like the chapter headings in a biography, but a long slow mutation of emotion, hidden, all-penetrative; [these inner changes are] something by which they are so taken up that the practical outward changes of their lives in the world, noted with surprise, scandal, or envy by others, pass almost unnoticed by themselves.

Nadine Gordimer

I have been talking, so far, about the kind of transition that is triggered off by a specific, external change and that represents the way that people deal with or get through the change. In other words, a change occurs, and then a transition takes place. Let's call this kind of transition a "reactive" transition. The transition after the death of my wife was reactive. The transition was a reaction to the change, and it was the path I took to get through the change.

But there is also another kind of transition, which I'll call "developmental." This is a transition which is not triggered by an external change but which is produced by a natural, inner unfolding of those aspects of ourselves that are built right into who we are and how we are made. The transition of adolescence is a developmental transition. So is the so-called midlife transition, and so is any profound shift to a new way of experiencing the world. Such awakenings can occur at any point in life—whenever one comes to a gradual or a sudden realization that one's career or marriage or lifestyle is no longer satisfying. A developmental transition can even be triggered simply by the recognition that there actually *are* alternatives to the status quo.

At such times, after being more or less the same person for months and years, it occurs to us one day that something has happened inside us. We may try to account for it by chalking it up to some event or blaming it on a change in someone else. But if we are honest with ourselves we can only say that things that used to mean a lot to us don't mean so much anymore, or that something that was once only a shadowy presence in our minds has taken the stage of our attention and demands our attention. We begin to wonder what life would be like if we did thus-and-so. We puzzle over we how we got to this point in our lives, what we really want out of life from this point forward.

The two different kinds of transition are characterized by the same three phases—an ending, a neutral zone, and a new beginning:

- In the ending, we lose or let go of our old outlook, our old reality, our old attitudes, our old values, our old self-image.[2] We may resist this ending for a while. We may try to talk ourselves out of what we are feeling, and when we do give in, we may be swept by feelings of sadness and anger. Why is this happening to me? My friends aren't troubled by such things!
- Next, we find ourselves in the neutral zone between the old and new—yet not really being either the old nor the new. This confusing state is a time when our lives feel as though they have broken apart or gone dead. We get mixed signals,

some from our old way of being and some from a way of being that is still unclear to us. Nothing feels solid. Everything is up for grabs. Yet for that very reason, it is a time when we sometimes feel that anything is possible. So the in-between time can be a very creative time too.

- Finally, we take hold of and identify with some new outlook and some new reality, as well as new attitudes and a new self-image. When we have done this, we feel that we are finally starting a new chapter in our lives. No matter how impossible it was to imagine a future earlier, life now feels as though it is back on its track again. We have a new sense of ourselves, a new outlook, and a new sense of purpose and possibility.

Feeling that way, we *may* decide to make changes in our lives. But whether or not a developmental transition leads to an actual external change, it leaves us feeling different inside.

• • •

Diseases almost always attack men
when they are exposed to a change.
Herodotus

I first discovered and came to understand the transition process not in the conceptual form that I am presenting here, but as an experience. It was 1974. I had left my career as a college teacher of American literature and had moved my family to the country. Both of those changes had occurred because Mondi and I had decided to join one of those "intentional communities" that were springing up in California at that time. Ours was formed by six families who had known each other well and had decided that it would be wonderful to live together in neighboring houses, with some shared facilities and frequent communal events.

I was very excited by the prospect of our new life, and we put a lot of planning into getting ready for the changes it entailed. There were many unknowns, of course, but I was expecting an exciting new adventure. And, as it turned out, it *was* exciting. But *I* was a mess! Within a month of making the move, I was being treated for a pinched nerve in my neck and elevated blood-pressure; I was also arguing all the time with Mondi, and I was feeling much more discouraged about the future than I had imagined I would be.

I kept telling myself: This is a *good* change, one that I wanted to make. I kept trying to convince myself that I was happy. If this is how a *good change* feels, I thought, what happens to you when you make a *bad* change? Body parts fall off, probably.

I worried that I had made a mistake coming out to the country. I also worried that I'd have to go back and beg to be rehired at the college where I had worked before our move. Not understanding the process of transition or knowing that endings can trigger off real mourning for what has been left behind, I could only imagine that the change had been a mistake: Why else would I feel so miserable?

The suffering caused by my ending felt something like a type of ritual that I had been reading about at the end of my teaching career. At that time, I had been reading less and less literature and more and more anthropology and psychology. (This is called "Not keeping up in your field.") One of the books that contributed to my "not keeping up" was an old book originally published in 1909 by a Dutch anthropologist named Arnold van Gennep. Called *Rites of Passage,* it was the first Western attempt to understand a widespread kind of ritual by which tribal groups helped their members negotiate the turning points in a lifetime—such as being born, coming of age, marrying, having a child, joining the circle of the elders and dying.[3]

These rituals had been separately studied before, but van Gennep was the first Westerner to realize that they were collectively similar and were, in fact, variations on a theme. He invented the term "rites of passage" to refer to them and noted that all of these rituals were ways of disengaging individuals from their old identities and helping them find new ones. All of these symbolic experiences started with an ending—some kind of ritual in which people were separated from their old worlds and the identities that they had in those worlds. The rituals also separated the people in passage from the way that they had been taught to understand reality. This type of ritual always finished with some symbolic way of reincorporating the people in transition into the social order, with new identities and new pictures of the world in their heads. In between the separation and the reincorporation, the people in transition were taken out into the wilderness and into a corresponding psychic in-between state that van Gennep called "the neutral zone."

We think of a coming-of-age ceremony as something that introduces young people to the adult life that they are entering, but van Gennep recognized that such a developmental shift would work only if they first let go of the childhood they were leaving. "You can't take it with you" applies in a figurative way to all of life's turning points, not just dying. You have to let go, to make an ending. To find the new, you must first relinquish the old. The great French scientist Claude Bernard made the same point when he said, "It is what we think we know already that often prevents us from learning."

I had always known that in rites of passage people were taught important elements of what the tribe viewed as "reality," but I didn't understand that this learning also required *unlearning* the "realities" they had been taught at an earlier point in their lives. And I had always dismissed tribal rituals as prerational magic, so it came as a shock to realize that they were better seen as a surprisingly sophisticated psycho-technology designed to move a person across the gap between one stage of life and the next. At the age of forty, when I left teaching, I was myself lost in one of those lifetime "gaps"—the so-called midlife transition. And, although my culture had no formal rituals for me to utilize, I was going through the very same three-part experience of ending, neutral zone, and new beginning that tribal people had ritualized. It was as though I were in an unritualized life-passage.

· · ·

The chief object of education is not
to learn things but to unlearn things.

G. K. Chesterton

You start with an ending: When I first moved to the country, I was dismayed to find that instead of feeling that my new life had started, I felt that my life was over. I was depressed and miserable. As much as I had wanted to leave teaching, I found that I missed the regularity of my old schedule and the familiar give-and-take of the classroom. I missed talking with colleagues about classes and gossiping about students. I missed the way my work had given me such a clear sense of who I was.

It was confusing to find that when I got to the country and into my tightly knit group of friends, the first thing I experienced was a painful sense of loss. That discovery puzzled others too; old friends and neighbors had seen me as this brave guy who was willing to walk away from a career that he no longer believed in. Now they were more than a little mystified when that same brave guy moped around and acted grief-stricken. They wondered if my behavior didn't just go to show that my big life-change had been a wrong turn. Maybe it had even been a sham. I have to admit that those suspicions occurred to me too.

One day shortly after we arrived at our community, Margaret, my youngest daughter, came home from the second grade to say that her teacher had asked all the students to find out what their parents were. She already knew that Mondi was a psychotherapist, but I . . . what was I? I groped for an answer, rambling on about doing some speaking and doing some writing and doing a lot of gardening and raising chickens. Margaret's eyes glazed over: She was looking for a noun—*teacher, farmer, doctor, waiter*—but the best I could give her was a string of participles: *doing* this and *doing* that. Participles didn't answer the question, *what are you*? I knew that even before I tried to foist them off on her, but I thought that maybe she wouldn't notice. She did.

It was only after I realized that the rites of passage began by separating the person from his or her old identity that I began to find meaning in my subjective experience of disidentification. In subsequent years I saw many clients struggling to make sense out of the same experience:

"I don't even know who I am any more without my job."

"If I'm not his wife, who am I?"

"The loss of our house in the fire made me feel as though I'd lost a piece of myself."

"With our last child off to college, we don't feel like the same people any more."

What I found in my own case was that it makes a world of difference if you think of disidentification as a first step in a process that will produce something new, rather than as the final step in the collapse of your whole life. That is why the passage-ritual model was useful. The idea of that ritual was to create a new identity, and the ending and the accompanying feelings of loss were only the ground-clearing operation that created the space for that new identity.

Back in 1974, the wisdom of making-endings-before-making-new-beginnings was being driven home to me in all sorts of ways. I had moved to the country partly because (as a professor of American literature) I had been infatuated with Thoreau's *Walden* and its story of living a basic life, close to nature. The heart of that undertaking, he had written, was to simplify your life. *Simplify, simplify, simplify!* he wrote. In retrospect, I can see that although I thought that this was what I was doing, I was really just trying to *add simplicity to my life.* In addition to all the old things I had been doing, I started heating the house with a woodstove and chopping wood for fuel and raising as much of the family food as I could and reusing everything over and over. Of course, my life grew more and more complicated in the process.

The unexpected discovery that you have to make an ending before you can make a beginning would have been less dismaying if I could have made a quick ending and then gotten on with a new beginning right away. But the new beginning I was looking for needed to include finding a new way to make a living, and that depended in turn on some new way of defining what kind of work I could do. Whenever I considered the work I could do, I thought of teaching literature, but that was what I wanted to *stop* doing. I had hit a serious impasse there.

What I was missing, of course, was that second phase of the passage experience: the neutral zone. (But I was in a hurry! I couldn't afford to spend months wandering around in the neutral zone, like some Aboriginal youth on a Walkabout. Besides I was a modern person, not a *primitive*.) In spite of my modernity, however, I slowly came to see that I needed to go through the wilderness phase of my transition, just as surely as did a native youth during his rite of passage. In tribal rituals, that wilderness was both inside and around the individual. That is, the youth spent time in the external wilderness because it represented the inner formlessness and confusion that comes when all the order provided by a "life" and an "identity" disappears.

That resulting state of chaos is not really a negative state or a breakdown of the way things are supposed to be, although it certainly felt that way to someone like me who didn't expect or understand it. It is actually a fertile state, a creative state, a state of pure energy and great potential. In the symbol-rich solitude of the traditional neutral zone, some god or spirit sent a dream or gave a sign to anyone who was in the midst of a passage ritual. The ancestors spoke or a totem animal appeared. In one way or another, people in passage discovered the clue that they needed to help them begin a new life. Of course, our society hadn't prepared me for my time in the neutral zone. Our language doesn't even have a term for that in-between time, and so it isn't surprising that I didn't have a practice of fasting or vigils or prayer to guide and support me.

But I came to see that those elements of ritual are merely the amplifiers of what goes on anyway. Human beings are wired to receive transition (or "passage") messages, even though the social broadcasting has ceased. That is why my time in the neutral zone had a profound effect on me, in spite of my limited understanding at the time. After my worst feelings of loss began to subside, something new started to emerge. It was an idea, very sketchy at first, for the kind of work that I could do. I began to think that the very experience I was having could be the subject of a new kind of assistance that I could provide people. I began to consider how I could work with people who were, like me, in transition.

To do that, I created a one-person educational enterprise called (in deference to my discoveries) "Passage-Ways" and started running

weekend seminars called "Being In Transition." They were modest
little undertakings, collections of ten or a dozen people with whom I
would discuss the three phases of transition and how it felt to experience them. I provided the expertise (which consisted largely of being
a page or two ahead of the group in the understanding of transition)
but I learned almost as much from them as they did from me. Each
time I ran a Being In Transition group, I understood a little more
about what transition was and what it did to a person's life.

•   •   •

*Oh, would that my mind could let fall its dead
ideas, as the tree does its withered leaves!*

André Gide

Twenty-five years later, I can look back and see that the reactive
transition I experienced after my career-change had actually been
preceded by a purely subjective (and, to others, invisible) developmental one that took place before I left teaching. That earlier time,
when I wasn't "keeping up in my field," was a time when I felt a
growing emptiness at the center of my life. It was a time of fantasies
about other lives that I might live. In retrospect, I could see that it
was that earlier transition that led me to leave teaching, to join the
six-family community, and to move to eighty-five acres of commu-
nally owned country land two hours north of San Francisco. Now I
can see that it had the same three phases that my later transition
would have.

Even before I left teaching, I had been separating myself from my
old life, just the way van Gennep had said that the first phase of a rite
of passage helped people to do. I had made an inner ending without
even knowing it. And well before I decided what to do and actually
stopped teaching, I was in the wilderness of the neutral zone just as
surely as if some initiation master had taken me out and left me
alone on a mountaintop. But it was an *inner* mountain top, an inner
wilderness. Outwardly, I went on with my regular activities. But be-

cause of my transition I was no longer the same person who had, only a few years earlier, loved teaching and suburban living.

I continued to go through the motions, all the while feeling utterly alone and bewildered. I spent two years in this "nowhere," puzzling over what to do. I regarded my dilemma as something I had brought on myself by . . . by . . . by doing (or not doing) I-didn't-know-what. It was only after that time in my inner neutral zone, when I found and joined the group that ultimately moved to the country, that I began to know again where I wanted to be and what I wanted to do.

In retrospect the three phases of transition look clear: My new beginning in the country community had been preceded by an inner experience of being lost, a bewildering neutral zone; and that experience came after I had let go of my old assumptions and outlook. That kind of naturally occurring inner transition leaves you feeling like a very different person, even though others may not notice the difference and even though you may not be able to name it—or even want to admit it to yourself. The old person that I had been before my transition would never have left a tenured teaching post and launched out on such an uncertain venture as did the new-person-I-had-become.

Now, twenty-five years later, I can say that a developmental transition led to a change, and that the change led to an reactive transition. I can readily see that they both had the same three-phase shape, and that their shape was the same as traditional rites of passage. But at the time, I was groping down a dark corridor of my life with only occasional glimmers of illumination. I was still distressed that I didn't know why I was feeling what I was feeling or where I was going to end up. I even felt guilty for having *changed*, as though my transition was a sign of some inner unreliability or shiftiness.

I'd like to be able to say that I saw what was happening as soon as I moved to the country, and that from then on I worked single-mindedly to reinvent myself. But the truth was that I was spending a lot of my time, in those days, trying to figure out how to recover the relative comfort and the security I had felt before I plunged into transition. I suspect that if anyone had offered to turn back the clock to the old days before I grew dissatisfied with teaching, I would have accepted the offer. I know now how common it is for people in transition to wish they could turn back the clock—and even to imagine that they are doing so, when what they are actually, if unwittingly, doing is moving forward toward something new.

It's an age-old story: You think that you are heading for India, and you end up in the West Indies. You run after the ball, and you fall down the rabbit hole. You're a prehistoric fish in a dried-up sea that's just trying to flop across the mud to a new puddle, and the next thing you know you're breathing air! You think that you are doing one thing, and all the time you are busy doing another. Many of the biggest transformations come when you think that you're just trying to reestablish the status quo.

·   ·   ·

There is a time for departure, even when there's no certain place to go.

Tennessee Williams

After I began to work with people in transition, I found that endings and losses are the commonest first sign that people are in transition. These endings tend to be signaled by one of several experiences:

- a sudden and unexpected event that—like Mondi's death—destroys the old life that made you feel like yourself;
- the "drying up" of a situation or a relationship that once felt vital and alive;
- an activity that has always gone well before, suddenly and unexpectedly goes badly;
- a person or an organization that you have always trusted proves to be untrustworthy and your whole sense of reality comes apart;
- an inexplicable or unforeseen problem crops up, at the worst possible moment, to disrupt the ordinary functioning of your life.

The irony is that people naturally view such events or situations as disasters to be averted, as problems to be solved, or as mistakes to be corrected. But since they are really signals that the transition process has commenced, making them go away is no more than turning off the alarm that woke you up.

Whatever its details, an outer loss is best understood as a surrogate for some inner relinquishment that must be made, but one that is difficult to describe. What it is time to let go of is not so much the relationship or the job itself, but rather the hopes, fears, dreams and beliefs that we have attached to them. If you let go only of the job or the relationship, you'll just find another one and attach the same hopes, fears, dreams and beliefs to it. And, on the other hand, you may find that you can let go of those inner attitudes without actually terminating the outer situation.

Since a loss is best seen as the cue that it is time to let go of the inner thing, one of the first things a person in transition needs to ask is: "What is it time for me to let go of?" The danger is that the person will fail to grasp the inner message and conclude that the outer change is the whole story. I myself had done that by believing that "moving to the country" and "finding a new career" were ends in themselves. Fortunately, my struggle took me long enough so that I had time to discover that what I had to let go of had far less to do with vocational activity and geography than with the programming that had carried me through the first forty years of my life.

When I say that a loss is a metaphor for an inner ending that it is time to make, I don't want to be misunderstood. I am saying that it is *as if* the outer loss was just a symbol. I'm not saying that you lose whatever you lose because someone (or Some One) is trying to teach you a lesson. "Why is this happening to me?" is no more enlightening a question when it is given a karmic twist than it is when you say it in a paranoid state. I am just saying to forget speculating about the identity of the sender and ("Hey, time to wake up!") read the message. I am saying that you can come out of an encounter with one of these ending-signals more effectively if you ask yourself what it is time to let go of.

But I am also saying a little more than that, because I have found that the best way to find meaning in an event or a situation is to regard it as though the event or situation were a person who was trying to get your attention. The setback caused by a loss is like the river that the hero encounters near the end of Herman Hesse's novel *Siddhartha*. The humble ferryboatman that Siddartha meets at the river's edge tells the hero:

> I have taken thousands of people across [the river], and to all of them my river has been nothing but a hindrance on their journey. They have traveled for money and business, to weddings and on pilgrimages; the river has been in their way and the ferry man was there to take them quickly across the obstacle. However, amongst the thousands there have been a few, four or five, to whom the river was not an obstacle. They have heard its voice and listened to it, and the river has become holy to them, as it has to me.[4]

Change can happen at any time, but transition comes along when one chapter of your life is over and another is waiting in the wings to make its entrance.[5] Needless to say, it is impossible to imagine a new chapter starting when your wife's death has just closed down what feels like your *whole life*. You simply cannot *imagine* a new chapter, but the fact is that letting go of one chapter in your life initiates the transition that concludes by beginning another chapter.

Transition does not require that you reject or deny the importance of your old life, just that you let go of it. Far from rejecting it, you are likely to do better with the ending if you honor the old life for all that it did for you. It got you this far. It brought you everything you have. But now—although it may be some time before you are comfortable actually doing so—it is time for you to let go of it. Your old life is over. No matter how much you would like to continue it or rescue it or fix it, it's time to let it go.

Whether letting go will be entirely subjective and internal or whether it will lead to further external changes may at first not be clear. Many people leap to the conclusion that "it is over" means that the life situation has to go. They get divorced. They walk out of the office, never to return. They leave the church. They abandon their education. They leave their country. They do these things, even though all that they were being called on to do was to leave the relation that they had had to these things. Even when the ending is literal, as it is in death, the most important relinquishment is not of the person but of the *life* that you shared with that person.

The relation between change and transition is further complicated by the fact that some people actually utilize external changes to distract them from the harder business of letting go of their subjective realities and identities. They make changes *so they won't have to make transitions.* They walk out on their marriages, but take along the attitudes toward partners that destroyed their marriages. Or they continue to search for "someone to take care of me" after they quit their jobs because their bosses are not interested in playing that role. Or they move because their town doesn't have any "interesting people" in it—only to find that their new town doesn't either. Such people may claim that they are "always in transition," but in fact they are probably never in transition. They are addicted to change, and like any addiction, it is an escape from the real issues raised by their lives.

It is the inner realities that are hardest to let go of. The Russian novelist, Leo Tolstoy, was talking about how and why we fail to make such inner relinquishments when he wrote:

> I know that most [people], including those at ease with problems of the greatest complexity, can seldom accept even the simplest and most obvious truth if it be such as would oblige them to admit the falsity of conclusions which they have delighted in explaining to colleagues, which they have proudly taught to others, and which they have woven, thread by thread, into the fabric of their lives.[6]

Tolstoy calls what people refuse to let go of their "truths" and their "conclusions." He might also have called them "outlooks" or "assumptions" or "realities." Those are the things that make people feel at home in the world because "they have [been] woven, thread by thread, into the fabric of their lives." People feel that walking away from them is walking away from life itself. Without them, the world would be strange and frightening. No wonder we hold on to them.

But until we let go of them, we are held in an enchantment. Like Sleeping Beauty, we are unaware of what is really going on around us. At first that unawareness may protect us, but one day it begins to close us down, to put us into a sleep, to wall us off from life. If we are lucky, a transition comes along to wake us up. If we are unlucky, we sleep through the rest of our lives.

•   •   •

One must be thrust out of a finished cycle in life, and. . . part with one's faith, one's love, when one would rather renew the faith and recreate the passion.

Anaïs Nin

I keep using the past tense to describe my insights into the transition process because they first occurred in the past. But when Mondi died, I wondered if I had really learned anything. After worrying about that for a while, I decided that the problem is with the very concept of "learning." In its commonest usage, the word refers to the acquisition of information. Once you have acquired the data, you are done with it once and for all: You then either know it or you don't. Discovering things about life doesn't fit that pattern, however. Whether you call them "truths" or something else, learning them involves discovering them again and again in different but similar contexts. Only then does the essential pattern imprint itself on your consciousness—although even then, it is dismayingly easy to lose sight of the pattern and be unable to find it again. Like a bird singing in a tree, it is there but not at the moment visible.

But life is generous. It keeps bringing us back for another look. The angle is always a little different. Sometimes the angle of vision breaks our hearts. That is how it was with my transitions before and after Mondi's death.

two

How I Rediscovered Transition

*How many times man lives and dies
Between his two eternities.*

William Butler Yeats

I don't believe that Mondi's illness and suffering were sent to teach her anything—or me, either, for that matter. But, together with her ultimate death, they did teach both of us a great deal. As she struggled along, day by day, for more than two years, she progressed from being simply a sick and frightened person to being someone who found a great deal of meaning in her sickness and uncovered new depths within herself because of her discoveries. And during that same time I progressed from being a stunned bystander, trying to understand what was happening, to being a participant in a profound and awe-inspiring experience. In the Christmas letter I wrote to family and friends seven months after she died, I said that the year of her death was the most wonderful year either of us had ever known.

Several months after she had been diagnosed with breast cancer, Mondi decided to write to her friends and update them on how she was doing. Two months later she wrote a second "update," as she began to call them. In these letters—fifteen of them before she died—she reflected on the experience of being very, very ill. She studied that experience in herself and in others who were affected by her condition, the way that a person might study life in a foreign country. If she was going to have to be there, she decided, she might as well find out as much as she could about what life was like in the Land of Dying.

Here is a passage from one of those updates. She wrote it about half way through her ordeal:

I really like new beginnings. I like the challenge of finding meaning in heretofore impossible situations. I like that Etty Hillesium could find hope and meaning by watching one little cloud, while she sat huddled in a Nazi concentration camp.[1] I like being in the middle of what's true and what's real, and what's at the center of things. I've always liked thinking about death, and I've always thought of death as a new beginning. Now I have to put my money where my mouth has always been. I accept that challenge. I'm willing to be awake and conscious if and when I become ill and die. For a person like me, who has such a strong interest in her spiritual development, having cancer is quite an opportunity. I also hate new beginnings. It is devastating to me to think of not seeing my children become middle-aged and my grandchildren grow up. It tears my heart apart to think of leaving Bill—he whom I have spent 37 years of my life with, for better and worse and everything else that happens in a good marriage. My friends are my treasures. I don't want to let them go. I don't know who I will be if I can't hike and run and ride my bike. It would be a terrible heartache not to be a Jungian analyst, after ten years of study and work towards that goal. How can I ever feel okay about leaving my patients, those who have trusted me so deeply and have risked their lives as they have counted on me? Who am I if I'm not a therapist? It's not that I don't think I'll still be here, therapist or not, but I'm just not too familiar with that non-therapist woman. And what about leaving this body? I've lived in it for fifty-six years, and it has served me so well. I don't know who I would be without this body, though I feel quite certain I'll still be me and I'll be around.

As a Jungian, Mondi had her own view of life's turning points, and while she had always been interested in my work with transition, my particular model of life-change was not the one she usually used to interpret her own experience. But as her situation grew more serious, she began to talk about her transition—or transitions, for once she began to look, she saw them everywhere. A year after writing the update I've quoted, she wrote this:

Cancer is okay if you like beginnings. Every day I have a new beginning. Every day I exchange who I thought I was for who I am now. I thought I was healthy; now I have cancer. I thought I had a treatable local recurrence; now it is most likely incurable metastatic cancer. For over 25 years I was a full-time therapist; now I am a part-time therapist. Today I'm writing a paper to become a Jungian analyst; next week I may have to go on a leave of absence to have a bone marrow transplant. Today my body feels strong and pain-free; in a month I may have the torture of chemotherapy. Today I'm a vigorous and involved grandmother who likes to take her grandchildren to Disneyland; next year I may be a grandmother who mostly looks on and delights in her grandchildren by watching and listening to them.

A mortal illness, she realized, is not just a lead-up to the big transition called "dying." There are beginnings and endings all the way along the path. You are constantly letting go of who you thought you were and how you thought life would be. You find yourself constantly in the neutral zone, unable to recover your old life but equally unable to embrace your new one comfortably. To the extent that you can let go of who you used to be and honor the experience of being in-between lives, you discover a rich and wonderful way of living. There is no beginning that doesn't require an ending, and no ending that doesn't make possible a new beginning.

Dying put Mondi under a bright light, and she began to see things that had always been shadowy before. In those days she saw, far more clearly than I then could, how life is made up of transitions at any level of detail you choose to look. I had tended to describe transition as a sometime thing, a state that a change has put you into. I realized intellectually that transitions were not limited to times of major change, that they were not just being born and dying, marrying and changing careers. But it was only through her that I saw the same pattern in all the tiny everyday relinquishments of our expectations and our hopes and all the little beginnings of some new way-things-are. She helped me to see the pattern in all the little neutral zones, when we are suspended for even a moment between a past that is gone and a future that we cannot quite yet see. Transitions are like those fractals in chaos diagrams, figures that replicate themselves at every level of magnification so that the parts take the same form as the whole, and the whole is present in each part.

In those days, Mondi's life was all transition. We had been told that the cancer probably wasn't very aggressive, but it kept growing. We were told that it was not very advanced, but it kept advancing. We were told that the lumpectomy had removed it and that the radiation had blitzed any cells that might have remained, but it came back. She had three cycles of chemotherapy, but none of the chemicals set it back more than momentarily. Hope and disappointment, hope and disappointment. All of her hair fell out twice. The cancer spread to the lung itself, and she had two painful operations to drain fluid that had started to build up there. She had to give up her work as an analyst and to say a wrenching good-bye to her patients. She had to stop doing almost everything that she loved to do, as the cancer moved through her like a dark rising tide.

As Christmas 1996 approached, she was in the hospital getting weaker every day, her lungs seriously damaged, and in constant pain. She had been an extraordinarily attractive, vivacious and athletic woman; but every week she grew thinner and weaker. There were times when she gasped for breath, and these times came more and more frequently. They put her on oxygen. Breathing hurt her so much that she needed morphine, and when breathing became very difficult she had panic attacks that left her groaning and pleading for help. Even with the oxygen and the morphine, she couldn't walk for more than twenty feet without stopping to rest.

Outwardly our lives were falling apart, but inwardly this began to be an extraordinarily rich time. Her days in the hospital gave us nothing but time to talk. I spent nights on a miserable little couch that unfolded into a miserable little bed. I, who had been so much slower than she was to admit that she was dying, now found it impossible to think of anything else. At the end of the day, I would lie beside her on her hospital bed, holding hands and talking, or hugging her and crying. We began to look forward to the evening, after she had taken her meds, when she was likely to feel fairly comfortable and the hospital was quiet—except for the man in the next room who screamed incoherently. He always served to remind us that it could have been worse.

I can't remember just when Mondi and I had started saying good-bye, but it was well before those days in the hospital. Once she was hospitalized and was so sick, all her energy went into survival and we stopped saying good-bye. But then, unexpectedly, she started to grow stronger again. At first it seemed too good to be true, but they finally said that she could go home—with the oxygen, of course. She would need that for the rest of her life, they said. So we went home and rigged up a bedroom in the main-floor study of our house. And we began saying good-bye again.

I remember wondering what we were doing and whether it was good that we were doing it. Some of the books that we read talked about keeping a "positive belief system," and they hinted that negative expectations were self-fulfilling. Saying good-bye, especially when she was obviously better than she had been, seemed several steps removed from a positive belief system, and we didn't do it as often any more. But every few days, one of us would simply be overcome by the sadness we felt when we thought that her reprieve might be only temporary, and we'd start our nighttime talks again. Always, they ended with her describing something that she wouldn't ever be able to do or see again. She would never take the last three of our five grandchildren to Disneyland for their fifth birthdays. She had loved that little tradition, both times she had done it, and the thought of losing it made her very, very sad.

We had some good times that spring, and there was even a period when we thought that the progress of the cancer had actually been reversed. As she got stronger, we began to try to work in as many good times as we could. She scheduled a trip to Disneyland with five-year-old Tristan, and we even managed to take a week-long trip to the Great Barrier Reef in Australia. But in that earthly paradise, at night as we lay side by side holding hands, we kept saying good-bye.

While we were there, her breathing began to get more difficult again. I read in one of her books about a Tibetan practice in which one concentrates during one's own in-breath on taking in a suffering person's pain, and during the out-breath on bathing the suffering one in love. I did that by the hour. Before the end of the trip, she had to check in to the little hospital in Cairns, Australia. The doctors were confused; perhaps she had developed pneumonia, or perhaps it was just the deterioration of her lungs.

"This positive-thinking stuff is crap," she said to me one evening as I sat on her hospital bed. "But then, so is negative thinking. They both cover up reality—which is that *we just don't know what is going to happen.* That's the reality we have to live with. But it is easy to see why people take refuge in optimism or pessimism. They both give you an answer. But the truth is that *we just don't know.* What a hard truth that is!"

Again, I was spending nights in the hospital, this time on the world's thinnest, most fragile folding cot. Finally, full of antibiotics for the pneumonia that she may (or may not) have had and terrified that the altitude on the flight home would make it impossible for her to breathe in spite of the oxygen tanks she was taking along with her, she had to fly back from the Australian trip alone while I finished up the work that had paid our way over there. Friends at home stepped in and took care of her for a week until I got back. I felt like a criminal for not being with her that week, but when I got back we had a great reunion.

She was obviously weaker, but having returned from the edge of death once, she had an air of invincibility about her. And she could always rise to an occasion. Our living room and kitchen were being remodeled—what kind of crazy timing was that?—so she entertained guests on the deck on the Sunday afternoon before she died. We had drinks and snacks, and she was very happy. But she overextended herself, and that night she had another long and terrifying bout of gasping and moaning for breath. Finally the morphine drops that she was now getting regularly took effect, and her rigid body relaxed on the bed. "That was a *bad* one," she said a little dreamily.

"It scared me," I said.

"I'm feeling better. Just stay with me."

"My God. Do you think I'm going to leave now?"

We both laughed.

"I don't want to go back to that damned hospital!"

"It'll be your choice."

"I have chosen." Then, amused by how that sounded, she said in a deep voice, "I HAVE CHOSEN!"

Two nights later we were lying in bed. Early in the day, she had had one of the little rallies that encouraged and confused us, but by afternoon the hospice nurse had had to come. Her breathing was shallow and difficult, and a crackling and popping accompanied each breath. The nurse increased Mondi's dose of morphine and started her on Ativan to calm the panic that set in each time she began to gasp for breath. The nurse left and she had several comfortable hours.

Then she had a terrible attack of breathlessness. I called the nurse and was told to triple her dose of morphine and double the Ativan. It took an agonizingly long time for the medication to take effect, and I couldn't do anything but hold her hand and talk to her. But finally it did take effect, calming her breathing again, and she dropped off to sleep. I put in a quick call to the nurse to ask if she thought I ought to call our three daughters and tell them to come home. She said that she would do that if she were in my shoes. As obvious as the signs were, I was shocked and frightened by her advice. Our daughters weren't surprised by the calls, however, and I found myself calmed by making them.

The narcotics made her drifty and she napped lightly. At supper time she felt well enough to talk to a friend for a few moments on the phone. From the next room, I could hear them laughing over some funny story. Later, as I got ready for bed, I gave her another dose of her medicine, wondering as I did so how people had dealt with these things before there were hospices. She would have been in the hospital, certainly, and miserable.

The evening was in many ways like others that spring. We were saying good-bye again. I thought back to those long early weeks when I had been unable to accept the seriousness of her disease, and I wondered how I could have been so blind and confused. I said, "I'll miss you so much!" and then I began to sob. After a few minutes during which we lay there holding hands and crying, we both calmed. Her breathing had been softened by the medicine, though her lungs still crackled in a way that scared me.

"Can you sleep?" I asked her.

"I think so," she answered.

We kissed. I put my arm around her neck. It was so skinny and wrinkled now. She turned toward me and curled up. She fell asleep suddenly, as she often did those days with the narcotics. I eased my arm out from under her head and got up.

I wandered around restlessly for a few minutes and then called our family doctor at home, feeling guilty as I did so for bothering him. He wasn't even the one who was treating her for the cancer, but he had promised to help however he could.

"Her breathing is very bad, Bob," I said, and I started to cry again. My crying came and went like something that had a life of its own.

"Just a minute," he said, "I have to change phones." I heard a TV sitcom filling up my ear with tinny laughter. Across the room, Mondi rattled like a machine that was shaking itself to pieces. On the phone,

Bob's voice called to someone to hang up the other phone. The tinny laughter stopped.

We talked briefly. I told him what was going on, but even over the phone he could hear her. He said he guessed that it would be no more than another day or two and that she would probably sleep for much of that time. I asked if there was anything more that we could do to make her comfortable. He asked about the doses of her medication, and when I told him, he said he thought that we were doing what she needed now. I thanked him and hung up the phone.

I went over to the bed and sat on the edge. I wanted to talk to her. Missing our evening talks, I went on solo. I told her that I guessed that the end was near. I was crying continuously now, and the crying felt as much a part of me as my heartbeat. I said that Anne and Sarah would be there soon and that I hoped that she could last until they arrived. Margaret had already come back from Virginia four days earlier to serve as a stand-in for Mondi on Tristan's long-awaited trip to Disneyland. When I had called her earlier in the evening, she had said she and Tristan would take the first available plane home. As if on signal, I heard a car stop up on the street and realized that she had just then driven up in a taxi.

Margaret and Tristan clumped down the stairs outside the room and the door opened. Margaret's voice was tense: "How is she, Dad?"

"She's having a really hard time, Mag."

Tristan pushed past her through the door and stood there silent and big-eyed and stiff.

"You can come in, Tris," I said. He did, but he never otherwise acknowledged my presence. His eyes were locked on Mondi.

She stirred in bed beside me, as though their mere presence had reached through the layers of her stupor. She opened her eyes and looked around in confusion. "Margaret and Tris are here to see you, sweetheart," I said.

Beside her, Tris whispered, "Hi, Nana."

With an enormous effort, she called back all her scattered attention and pushed herself up a little higher on her pillows. "Oh, hi,

Tris." There were long pauses between her phrases. "What was the best ride?"

"The Spinning Tea Cups, I guess," he whispered hoarsely.

Then to me: "Can I have more morphine soon?"

"I'll get it now." I brought over a dropperful and squeezed the bitter liquid into her mouth. She made a face and settled deeper into the pillows. Then, almost as an afterthought, she blew me a kiss.

She never woke again. Anne and Sarah, together with the remaining grandchildren, drove up half an hour later. They sat beside her and held her hand and talked to her, but she was too far away to acknowledge their presence. Then they went into the other bedrooms where the sleepy children were put to bed. It was midnight.

I can't remember what I said to Mondi for the next few minutes, but I remember that it suddenly occurred to me that she used to ask me jokingly, "Why don't you ever sing to me?" Her tone of mock dismay always suggested that most other husbands sang to their wives pretty regularly. I thought back over her favorite songs, but nothing seemed quite right.

Then it came to me. One of our first real dates had been in New York when we went to the musical comedy *The Music Man*. So I began to sing softly the love song from that show:

> Goodnight, my someone, goodnight, my love.
> Sleep tight, my someone, sleep tight, my love.[2]

Her breathing rasped and rattled, as though some inner creature, craving freedom, were shaking its chains. She lay propped up, gaunt and pale in the moonlight from the window. If I squinted, she looked almost as young as the slender nineteen-year-old I had fallen in love with all those years ago. But the hand I held was immeasurably old. Her bony chest rose and fell as she worked so hard to breathe.

Sarah came back into the room. Anne and Margaret were talking with the grandchildren. I left Mondi with Sarah and went outside alone for a few minutes. The spring night was so calm and lovely that it was hard to remember what was going on inside. Thirty-seven years together, and now only a day or two more!

I went back into the bedroom where Sarah was holding Mondi's still hand. She said that she was going to look in on the children, but that afterwards she would come back and sit for a while. When she left, I slid into the bed beside Mondi. I put my arm under her head. She was warm, and I found myself thinking that her death might not be so near as we were imagining. At the same time, it really didn't matter any longer. I felt enormously tired and strangely empty.

Without any particular forethought, I began to talk to her. I told her how brave I thought she had been throughout the two-year ordeal. I told her how sorry I was for having taken such a long time to accept the reality of her cancer and to help her in her struggle. I thanked her for giving me a great lesson in how to die and told her that when my time came, I would try to remember how she had done it.

I said that I thought our three girls—grown women, but still "our girls"—were in pretty good shape and that she did not have to worry about them. I said that I too was going to be all right and that it was time, now, for her to look after herself because that immense next step in her life journey, whatever it was like, would require all her energy and attention. I kissed her and stroked her face, then snuggled up against her narrow body. In a few minutes, I half-heard Sarah come back in, but I didn't hear when she left.

When I awoke in three hours, it was still dark but the predawn birdsongs had started. It took me a minute to realize that Mondi's noisy breathing had stopped. I put my hand on her chest. Her body felt warm, so she could not have been dead for long. But she was gone. Off somewhere else, away on other important business.

•   •   •

Observe constantly that all things take place by change, and
accustom thyself to consider that the nature of the universe loves
nothing so much as to change the things which are.

Marcus Aurelius

Once again, there they were—those damned three phases of transition. There was the letting go that she had fought against for a long time and I fought even longer. But when we did let go of the blind and thoughtless struggle, we found ourselves in a strange place that neither of us had known existed. It was like those dreams where you unexpectedly find a room in your house that you hadn't known was there. This place was the neutral zone—no doubt about it. That in-between time was very special.

At first it was fearful to her, but slowly she explored it and found that it was not such a bad place to be. Here is how she described it in one of her last updates:

For many days after my surgeries, I lay in an in-between zone. I could see life and I could see death. I felt drawn toward both but was very content to be where I was. The in-between zone is not a painful place. It reminds me of somewhere I used to go at Playland at the Beach. In the Fun House they had a huge disc on the floor that spun. When it stopped, all of us children ran and sat on it. As it began to spin we would be whirled off the disc. Only the person at the center would stay on until the operator stopped it from spinning.

For several weeks I felt like I was lying at the center of the disc. It would have been easy to go off in either direction. What was painful was when I could not accept the possibility of my death. I was agonized and tortured when I refused to accept that I might not see my grandchildren again. Or that perhaps Bill's body would never be entwined around mine. That I would never work with my patients again. That I might never chase my dog, Emma, around the house in pursuit of a snuggle. That I'd never watch the trees outside my windows or walk on Stinson Beach again. That I'd never hear Anne, Sarah or Margaret say, "Hi Mom!"

I've worked hard to have the family and life-style I have. It seems so special to me. And it is so easy to be caught up by how special my life is. And then, just as I begin to feel so proud of myself, I remember that there are billions of other "special" people in the world with their "special" lives. I have to laugh at myself. Mine is really no different from anyone else's except that it's mine. On a sidewalk in San Francisco today I saw a black woman holding the hand of her eight year old son. They were smiling at one another and giggling. How special. But then everything is special. I'm looking outside at a pine tree as I write. It has zillions of needles, each special and each just like all the others. I find an odd comfort in realizing that I'm just one of humanity's needles—nothing special. It helps me accept the passage of life and the movement towards my death.

When I am caught up in this world, it seems abhorrent to think of leaving my loved ones. From the in-between world, where I was for so long, it does not feel so bad. I fear I will offend some people when I say this, but I also hope to offer some relief. It was enormously relieving to me to look at death on one side of me, and life on the other and to be able to smile at each one. It was relieving to know that I could say good-by to my husband, friends, analyst, relatives, dog, house. (I almost said "my" mountains and "my" sky.) They would be okay and I would be okay. I had never guessed this psychological space existed. It was very reassuring.

The endurance of terrible pain and the proximity to my own death pushed me into the in-between world. There is such a clutching and clawing to stay in this world—just the way I have known it. It is so seductive. It's impossible to believe that there is anything else. I am so grateful I was able to get to an acceptance of whatever was next, and I relaxed and felt at peace. I liked to just look out the window and watch it rain for hours at a time. Whatever was going to happen felt okay.

What Mondi called her "in-between world" had two faces. Seen from one side, it was confusing, incomprehensible, even terrifying. Seen from the other, it was the still center of the spinning Playland disc, a place where you could lie and watch, a state of being in which you could discover another reality. That time in the in-between world brought her insights that she had never had before and gave her the words to speak and write as she had never done before. But it also terrified her. The in-between world granted us more intimacy and joy than we had ever had together before. Yet the clock was also at one minute to midnight, and we both knew it.

three

Why We Go Through Transition

Everybody wants to be somebody; nobody wants to grow.

Goethe

In its most basic function, transition helps you come to terms with change. It reorients you so that you can mobilize your energy to deal successfully with your new situation—whether it is a "good" one or a "bad" one doesn't matter—instead of being hampered by attitudes and behaviors that were developed for and more appropriate to your old situation.

In 1974, when I left college teaching and moved to the country, I was dealing with this aspect of transition, and it is the kind of transition that I have been helping companies deal with for the past twenty years, by showing managers how to help people reorient themselves after a merger or a reorganization. It is the kind of transition that people must make when they move to a new country, a new city, or even a new neighborhood. It involves relinquishing the old habits and expectations and developing new ones that fit the new situation.

When I started my new career leading transition workshops, I focused most of my energy on creating the workshops and relied on newspaper announcements about them to gather my clientele. In my heart I was still a college teacher, seeing myself as a developer and deliverer of ideas. I didn't think of myself as someone whose task was to convince people to attend the class. (At college, that job belonged to the admissions director, the dean, the advisers, and the registrar.) It isn't surprising that my early independent seminars were *very* sparsely attended! I had to shift my self-image, my behavior and my whole outlook to make a go of my new work. And that transition took a lot longer than the changes that I made to launch the seminars in the first place.

It didn't help that I came from a long line of teachers and had been raised to regard business as only a little higher on the ethical scale than prostitution. The reality was that over the next several years I had to create a business to deliver those seminars, and to do that required me to let go of my whole pseudo-ethical ranking of human activities that put me-as-a-teacher on a special rung near the top. I had to let go of my old habits, had to stop expecting my interesting ideas themselves to draw people, and had to start building the market for my programs.

I also had to develop a whole new way of running the seminars. As a teacher, I had always enjoyed creating my courses afresh each fall, but when I tried to do the same thing with my weekend seminars, I found that inventing a new program each week wore me out. Changing the workbook and the class exercises over and over again was just too much!

I can remember vividly the day I first decided to create a standardized, formally printed workbook that would stay the same for *a whole year!* The idea seemed inevitable, but doing it felt like selling out. I had never known how much of my pride and self-image was tied up in being a teacher who was always improving his teaching materials. If I let go of that way of doing things, I felt that I'd be cutting corners and short-changing my clients. (See, business *was* a form of prostitution!)

But it was even worse than that, for I ended up actually paying someone to do a computer-based layout of my materials so that they wouldn't look so much as though they had been done for a seventh-grade class project. ("It's the intellectual content that counts," said my old teacher-self scornfully. "How things look is just superficial." Then that inner monitor added, "You aren't going to try to get by with slick appearances, are you?") I gave in with a heavy heart and grave misgivings.

Reorientation is transition's essential function, even in matters of life and death. Mondi was continually having to reorient herself as she got sicker, and her death required the greatest reorientation I had ever made—one that is still, three years later, going on.

•   •   •

The important thing is this: to be able at any moment to sacrifice what we are for what we could become.

Charles DuBos

As critical as *reorientation* is to your understanding of the world and your practical engagement with it, focusing entirely on it makes being in transition a more superficial process than it actually is. The situation changes and *then* you react—which makes transition into a game of catch-up. In that case, you would be like my little dog, Emma, who loves to walk on the beach with me, lagging farther and farther behind as she is tantalized by wonderful smells—until she suddenly realizes that I am getting away, and comes galloping after me. In this routine of lag-behind-and-then-dash-to-catch-up, transition is just the accelerated movement that makes up for our slower motion at other times. As useful and necessary as that is, if that were all that transition did I wouldn't be writing and you wouldn't be reading a book on the subject.

One thing that the reorientation function doesn't account for is that in reorienting ourselves, we also have the chance—although it is optional whether or not we seize it—to take a step forward in our own development by letting go of a less-than-adequate reality and an out-of-date self-image. So the second function of transition is *personal growth.*

The Bible says that when we were children, we understood as children and thought as children and saw as children, but that when we became adults we "put away childish ways." Forget for the moment that people don't automatically do that— in fact, many people hold on to some of their childlike patterns of thinking and feeling long after they've grown up. The point is that we *can* let them go and, further, that transition is an invitation for us to do so.

You might wonder why we even need transition to reorient us and allow us to develop. Why can't we keep making little day-by-day and minute-by-minute changes? We've all heard that change is a constant today, so why aren't we constantly changing? The answer is that in physical ways we are, but that we don't—and *can't*—keep up with those external changes and modify our self-images bit by bit, moment by moment. To do that would require a constant updating process that would take up most of our energy as it forced us to question constantly every element of our lives.

Even though every new day is (as the cliché puts it) *the first day of the rest of our lives,* it is not really practical to do a whole, from-the-ground-up reinterpetation of reality every morning before we get out of bed. We don't start our lives all over again from scratch hour by hour. We take things—about the world and about ourselves—as givens until they prove to be false. Fortunately for us, we can go along for a good while before our perceptions get out of touch with external reality enough that we really have to abandon and replace them.

It is common to stick with the old reality until some kind of change comes along and jars our whole inner world out of its old alignment. At such times we are plunged into transition. It is all the more profound, then, because in a sense we are *ripe* for the experience because we are a little (in some cases, *a lot*) behind the curve of our own development. My move to the country was like that: a kind of a "timely" disruption of my life that made it possible for me to catch up outwardly with my inner life. As I said earlier, I had been finding less and less meaning in my old career and trying to find a path into a new one for several years. I was, you might say, running a "transition deficit," and that made the transition even more necessary, as well as more profound. And as I was to find, this was also true in the case of Mondi's death.

Transition can go a step further than personal growth, although the likelihood that it will is even less automatic than growth is. Transition may not be simply a step toward an outlook that is more appropriate to the life-phase that we are actually in. It can also be a step toward our own more *authentic* presence in the world. That would mean that we come out of a transition knowing ourselves better and being more willing to express who we really are, whenever we choose to do so. It would also mean that we are more often willing to trust that who-we-really-are is all right—is valid and a person capable of dealing with the world.

A middle-aged man who enrolled in one of my early transition seminars was trying to decide what to do after a reorganization at his law firm left him with more power but less interesting work than he had had before. In talking about what he might do, he suddenly started talking about another turning point in his life—when he had been nineteen and had given in to his father's pressure to go into the law. His alternative, he said with a faraway look, had been to be a classical musician. "I probably wouldn't have been a really good one," he said, "but music sure made me happy!"

As we talked, I could see that the person this man was when he was being most himself was not a lawyer. Hard as he had worked at his profession, it had never stirred him or expressed anything significant about him. He was fortunate, because he had worked long enough to save the money he would need to retire from the law and take the momentous step of following a path that had only his own authenticity to justify it. When I last heard about him, he was happily playing in a small regional symphony orchestra.

It is unlikely that either *development* or *authentication* would occur if it were not for a further characteristic and function of transition, which is that it gives us access to the wellsprings of our own *creativity*. When the young member of a tribe was taken out into the wilderness to fast and chant and pray, it was said that he or she gained access to the guidance of the gods or to the spirits of the ancestors or to the voices of the tribe's totem animals. To translate that into a little more modern and less culturally specific terms, you could say that in transition—and specifically in the neutral-zone phase of transition—people gain access to their deeper creative energies and impulses.

As products of a society that does not send people out on vision quests, we may feel that this idea of access to creative "voices" is far removed from our own tradition or the world that we live in. But in both the Old and New Testaments there are numerous accounts of people who are in transition getting a visit from an angel or having a dream in which God speaks to them. Jacob, at a turning point in his own life, encountered a nighttime angel who wrestled with and injured him. And changed him too, as encounters with our inner creative agents usually do.

Remember too that modern research on creativity finds that unexpected solutions to difficult problems and creative ideas in general come out of a murky state where purpose and focus are temporarily suspended—a state very much like what we are calling the neutral zone. It's also worth noting that many of the decisions that change the direction of our lives are made during in-between times, after something has ended but before our lives have taken a definitive new shape.

In the neutral zone a person enters a realm where anything can happen. Whatever the change that triggered the transition was meant to produce, the neutral zone opens up a world of utter possibility. That is why many people find being in such a state so disconcerting. In changes where the outcome cannot be foreseen—where there is just an ending and a neutral zone that stretches beyond the horizon—this state of possibility can be quite terrifying. But in such cases, transition's *creative* function is even more critical, for it is only by exploring the neutral-zone experience with an open mind that people can *create* a satisfactory outcome to the change. It is only when they have done so that they have a good chance to make the beginning that will take them into the next leg of their life-journey and the next chapter of their development.

Reorientation, personal growth, authentication and creativity: What these four things have in common is that they all require that you let go of the way that you have experienced your work and yourself. When you've done that, you drift for a while, open to the insights and the promptings from your own inner voices. At such times you can often find significance in the chance patterns and synchronistic events around you. Many of the tribal practices during passage rituals are simply ways of endowing these timely happenstances with significance and giving them more weight.

Through reorientation, personal growth, authentication, and creativity, our lives decompose and then recompose around a new theme or idea. *Reorientation* refers to that process as a turning in the way we go through life. *Personal growth* refers to the way reorientation brings us into a new and more adequate relationship to the world around us. *Authentication* refers to the inner face of growth, where the result is not just appropriate but is also some way of being that is truer to who we really are, rather than to a persona or a role.

Each of these functions grows out of the *creative* opportunity that comes to us in the form of "the chaos" or "the empty field" or "the fallow time" (there are many metaphors) of the neutral zone. Each of these metaphors is simply a way of framing the confusion and the up-in-the-air quality that most people experience there. Each is a different way of saying that it is the nothingness that we find there that gives the neutral zone its power, not *something* that we encounter in that in-between state.

·   ·   ·

Only a life lived in a certain spirit is worthwhile. It is a remarkable fact that a life lived entirely from the ego usually strikes not only the person himself, but observers also, as being dull.

C. G. Jung

There is also a fifth function that the tribal groups, with their walkabouts and vision quests, would have said was central to the whole rite of passage experience, but which many modern people find it difficult to talk about or even believe in when they encounter. That is the *spiritual* function of transition. The religious historian Mircea Eliade was speaking of this function when he said that tribal groups believe that passage rituals connected their participants with a timeless state out of which the world emerged—a state that Eliade called The Sacred.[1] It is in the neutral zone that we can most readily encounter The Sacred.

Most people today imagine that spirituality and The Sacred have something to do with religion—which is to say, with an organized body of belief and some institutional tradition which acts as the repository and defender of that heritage. But the sacred realm that Eliade was talking about and to which I refer here doesn't belong to any religious body. It is a natural, but often overlooked, dimension of living itself. It is a way of experiencing the world (so the ancient traditions claimed) that one could enter through special entry-points within nature, the cycle of the year, or the course of a lifetime. These points of access are like spiritual doorways through which one could "cross over," sometimes unaware, into a whole different way of seeing and understanding the world.

Tribal groups often located these doorways in specific geographical places that they considered to be holy places:

- On mountaintops, like Mt. Sinai or Mt. Olympus or a thousand lesser-known spots, where the earthly plane of experience rises up into the heavens and provides access to the world of spirit. Almost every tribal group that lives around mountains has a special high-point of access to the spiritual world.
- In the desert wilderness, where Jesus went for a period of solitude, introspection and self-discovery. The so-called Desert Fathers continued that tradition monastically in Christianity for hundreds of years, and many people today

instinctively feel the special "power" of the desert when they are alone in it. There the absence of leafy life can leave one in a blank and receptive state, like the proverbial clean sheet of paper on which nothing has been written.

- Beside a well or spring, a natural point of access to the spirits of the earth and the wisdom that they carry. (Lest you think that this is just a "pagan" idea, recall how often significant events occur at wells in the Bible and how many springs are sacred to some particular saint in Europe.) The point at which life-giving water rises up out of the earth is a natural metaphor for the point at which the sacred breaks through the crust of the profane.

- At a singular geographical feature or within a special land-scape where one goes to encounter the sacred. Such a place is Uhuru, the vast monolith that whites used to call Ayers Rock in the central Australian outback. Other cultures have lo-cated their sacred space in deep stretches of forest—a tradi-tion that comes down to us in the enchanted forests or goblin-filled woods of Western fairy tales.

- Some site made sacred by its association with spiritual power or the manifestation of holiness at some time in the past—Jerusalem or Mecca or Glastonbury. We can feel echoes of this sacredness even in places unrelated to holi-ness, if they are associated with deep sacrifice: The battle-field at Gettysburg and the Vietnam Veterans Memorial in Washington, D.C., come to mind.

In any of these places, one could, with luck, encounter the other di-mension of life that is the sacred and the spiritual.

But all of these places are simply the physical symbols of—or im-ages that evoke, or triggering mechanisms for—what is a natural state of mind that in the right circumstances any of us can enter into. And it is that state of mind that we are most likely to encounter in a neutral zone. You yourself have probably had the experience, al-though since we lack a tradition of cultivating such experiences and a language for talking about them, we often dismiss them as weird or even pathological. Without a way to make sense out of such experiences, we often protect ourselves by saying that they are imaginary.

Besides these five ways in which transition serves us, there is also a sixth function that integrates them all. Transition *renews* us. It is as though the breakdown of the old reality releases energy that has been trapped in the form of our old lives and converts it back into its original state of pure and formless energy.

It is recapturing that energy that permits us to be reborn anew— as in the old rites of passage, the person was put through a symbolic experience of being was born all over again. Transition brings us back to the initial moment of creation, for as Rabbi Zalman Schachter-Shalomi notes, the "In the beginning" of Genesis 1:1 ought really to be translated as "In *a* beginning." The Beginning at the start of the Bible is really any beginning, any moment of creation. All beginnings come from situations that are "without form and void."

· · ·

Every beginning is a consequence—
every beginning ends something.

Paul Valéry

As in so many other ways, the ancient traditions grasped a truth that we have largely forgotten. That truth is that renewal comes neither by taking a rest nor changing the scenery, nor by adding something new to our lives, but by ending whatever is, and then entering a temporary state of chaos when everything is up for grabs and anything is possible. Then—but only then—can we come out of what is really a death-and-rebirth process with a new identity, a new sense of purpose, and a new store of life energy.

Renewal is much more like going from fall through winter to spring than it is like taking a vacation from school or work or treating ourselves to something special. That is why our impulse to get something new (a car, a lover, a house, or a piece of clothing) so often leads not to renewing our lives but to yet another experience of dissatisfaction and disappointment. Renewal is possible only by going into and through transition, and transition always has at least as much to do with what we let go of as it has with whatever we end up gaining in its place.

And just what is it that one has to let go of to benefit from this renewing transition? That is something that cannot be described in the abstract, nor is it likely to be knowable in advance. If the ending is accompanied, as mine was, by a traumatic loss, it is obvious that you must let go of that particular relationship. But it is, as I discovered, only as you go into the ending that life sets before you do you find out what else it is time to let go of. That is why the religious counsel to give up this or that particular thing is no more than a handbook sketch to help you to recognize your own particular relinquishment when you happen to come upon it.

•   •   •

The whole life of the individual is nothing but the process of giving birth to himself; indeed, we should be fully born, when we die, although it is the tragic fate of most individuals to die before they are born.

Erich Fromm

These six functions of transition are easiest to recognize in a situation where a change has jarred us out of our comfortable identification with the circumstances that have surrounded our lives and triggers off what we have been calling a reactive transition. The change itself alerts us to the transition. The change helps us to "unplug" ourselves from our everyday lives. But in the purely inner process that we are calling a developmental transition the six functions of transition also occur. Whether that kind of transition is gradual or sudden, we find that our old life no longer makes sense or gives us the satisfaction that it used to. In that realization, the emotional connection to our old life is broken.

In such cases, however, there is no change to serve as a signal that something important has happened. Because the challenge we face is purely subjective, it is not likely to call forth a plan the way an external change does. So we lack a road map by which we can track our progress. We do not have anything to prepare for or any future to adjust to. We have only the gradual (or sudden) discovery that our lives, as we have been living them, aren't workable or livable as is any longer.

In my own case, I discovered that I was in this kind of transition when I slowly acknowledged to myself that the teaching career I had been so devoted to had gone dead in my late thirties. In another person's case, it might be a marriage that was discovered to be no longer sustainable or a circle of friends and a lifestyle that had come to seem empty and hollow. Whatever the details, a developmental transition is invisible to others until you talk about it or until its impact upon you is so strong that you decide to make an external change because of it.

Why transition happens when it does is at one level a mystery, but in another sense it is not so difficult to explain. As we move through life, we extrude the world we live in, in the same way that a crustacean grows its shell—for protection. I am not saying that the world doesn't have important elements that are objective. Just that it is so colored by how we experience it—and that that experience is so individual—that it is difficult to know how much we create and how much we encounter.

Our reality and the "world" that went with it fitted us when we first discovered them, but as time passes the protective shell begins to be limiting and to cramp us. When our reality and our sense of who we are starts to get old in this way, we usually try to find ways to fix things and put them back the way they were. We imagine that there is something we could add or do differently. We may spend a great deal of time, energy and money on those attempts, but at last we have to acknowledge that all the king's horses and all the king's men won't be able to put *this* Humpty together again.

In some cases, people tire of the arrangements of their lives and the details of their reality and initiate the ending themselves, but it is probably more common for something to break in on them from outside and destroy the conditions of their lives, even though they have no conscious desire for that to happen. But in either case, transition comes along when it is time for people to get back into synch with how things really are. Take note: I am not saying that *the change* comes along to get you back into synch. The change comes along for its own reasons, but when it triggers off a significant transition, it does so because there is some reorientation or development that needs to take place.

Some people fight transition all the way and bewail their fate, while others come to recognize that letting go is not defeat—that it may, in fact, be the start of a whole new and rewarding phase of their lives. As the American writer Margaret Halsey wrote, "In some circumstances, the refusal to be defeated is a refusal to be educated." Why is it that way? *Because*, that's why.

Even death, as Ram Dass told Mondi and me when he came over to our house one day to talk to her about her cancer, is really a lot like taking off a pair of too-tight shoes. The most we can say when we are faced with the mystery that is at the heart of the transition process is that when we find ourselves in transition, life is telling us that it is time to let go of what we have been holding on to. It is time—life says it—to go into the neutral zone and out of its state of pure energy that we call "chaos"—to discover or create a new way of being and a new identity.

In the past twenty-five years, there have been a number of books that purported to explain the timing and the outcome of our life-transitions. Starting in the mid-seventies with Gail Sheehy's *Passages: The Predictable Crises of Adult Life*, Daniel Levinson's *The Seasons of a Man's Life* and Roger Gould's *Transformations: Growth and Change in the Adult Years*, such books have charted out a sequence of "stages" through which adults were said to progress. But although some people found their own experiences reflected in these timetables, many did not. Further, the transition process, as presented in these model itineraries, was only the way that you got from one life-phase to the next, a period of turmoil while life was changing the scenery on the stage of your play.

As I worked with people during those same years, I came to a different conclusion. It was transition that was the important fact, because it was transition, not the stages, that reoriented and developed us—as well as giving us access to our authentic selves, our creativity and a deeper level of spiritual significance in our experience. I came to see that the stages were just the natural and temporary resting places between transitions—and further that they were far more various and unique to particular individuals than the books were saying. It was the transitions that were alike, across many different personal contexts; it was the transitions that did the heavy lifting of growth and development. The stages were simply the necessary times during which we could incorporate and consolidate the discoveries made and the power released in the transitions.

•   •   •

Life does not accommodate you, it shatters you. . . Every
seed destroys its container or else there would be no fruition.

Florida Scott-Maxwell

Although some transitions result from changes that were undertaken in hopes of producing some particular outcome, they often transform us in ways that we cannot foresee. Transition has a will of its own, and we come out of transition in ways that cannot be known in advance. That happens when we go to college, when we get a new job, or when we buy a bigger house. Each of these is a desirable change, and we undertake them all with some positive outcome in mind.

But each of them is also guaranteed to initiate a transition that will force us to let go of how our lives have been: We may be separated in the process from friends or estranged from a sibling or a parent who feels that we are abandoning the family or the neighborhood—even that we are just trying to be "different" or that we're turning into a "big shot." The losses are natural by-products of transition, although no one warns us about them when we were considering making the change.

Transition may also, of course, bring us very positive new beginnings that were also unforeseen when we initiated the change. We may gain skills and knowledge that bring great pleasure, friendships that change our whole lives and new interests that form the basis of our hitherto unimagined careers. But however things turn out, transition is more than simply how we get from to *here* to *there*, because it also often presents us with a *there* that we did not expect—a *there* that is shaped by the creative and developmental functions of the transitional journey itself.

A memorable example of transition having a will of its own occurred during one of my transition seminars that was incorporated into an Outward Bound raft trip on Utah's Green River. Besides the singles, there were three couples on the trip (Mondi and I were one of them). On the first night the Outward Bound guides asked all the couples to split up and ride in separate boats. That way, they explained, everyone would have a powerful individual experience, undistorted by relationship issues that we might happen to be dealing with.

We and one of the other two couples agreed to ride in separate rafts. But the husband of the third couple argued: His wife was shy and fearful, he said; she wouldn't be comfortable being alone with people she didn't know; he was coming on this raft trip partly to expose her to something new and exciting; but, hey, there were limits to what he wanted to put her through. She sat there silently in her not-very-outdoorsy clothes and smiled at him gratefully.

Later in the evening, the guides explained how the trip would be run. After some basic instruction the next morning, we'd split into boat crews. There would be an Outward Bound staff member in each boat, but that person wouldn't captain the raft. Instead, one of the participants would captain the raft for each half day, and that way there would be at least one significant rapids for each of us to navigate. Again the husband spoke up: The Little Lady would pass on that one too, he said. It was just a little too scary. The trip itself was a big challenge, and he was real proud of her [he looked at her proudly] for doing it at all. But captaining down a rapid . . . No, they'd skip that part, thanks just the same. The rest of us looked at his wife discretely to see if she was comfortable with this kind of protection. She just smiled deferentially.

The four-day trip was a great adventure down a challenging river in a stunningly beautiful canyon. The high point for most of us was the few intense hours that each of us spent bellowing *right, left, back, forward—hard!* and the anxious excitement we each felt as we tried to position our raft at the top of a big rapid in such a way as to miss that darned huge rock right in the middle—the one with the awful sucking sound beyond it. On the last day of the trip, each raft had just one remaining person who had not captained yet, and they all got into place for our last adventure—except, of course, for The Little Lady.

Just before we started down that final rapid, an argument broke out on that couple's raft, but since theirs was the last raft in our group, we were soon out of earshot and couldn't learn what was going on. My raft was the one directly ahead of theirs, so when we pulled up to the other rafts in the quiet water after running the last rapids, I turned back and saw an amazing sight. The final raft was coming down—not always pointed forward and hitting a lot of rocks as it barreled through . . . but with The Little Lady calling out commands in a surprisingly loud voice.

Everyone was speechless. As the raft drifted up to us, we sat there silently as she called on her crew to *back-water*. The raft turned slowly and bumped to a rest against ours. The Little Lady was breathing heavily, although her husband looked as though he had stopped breathing some time ago. "Well!" she said in the voice of someone who had just made up her mind about something. "When we get back to the cars, I'll be looking for a ride back to Denver! Any offers?"

Accomplishing something will often trigger a transition. Sometimes the result is what we hoped for and sometimes it isn't, but in either case, the result comes about because achieving the result necessitates not only a situational shift (a change) but an inner redefinition. At the very least, the person lets go of the idea of doing thus-and-so and turns into the person who actually did thus-and-so. And as the river trip taught us, the transition can go way beyond any intended results.

•   •   •

*Each man's life represents a road toward himself, an attempt at
such a road, the intimation of a path. No man has ever been
entirely and completely himself. Yet each one strives to become
that—one in an awkward, the other in a more intelligent way,
each the best he can.*

Hermann Hesse

Because transition is the six-function dynamic that moves us forward along the path toward becoming ourselves, the story of a person's transitions is much closer to the essential pattern of his or her own life history and path of development than any general theory of life stages can ever be. But the story of your transitions, taken by itself, does not speak of your developing or of becoming more authentic, any more than the transitions themselves can be guaranteed to leave you with those gifts. It is only when each transition has been reflected upon and understood, does it disclose a personal "developmental task" embedded in it. And only then can you identify its significance as a turning point in your personal path.

As I said earlier, one of the best ways to approach any transition is to ask, "What was it time for me to let go of at that point in my life?" Let me use my own career change in 1974 to illustrate how you might ask that question and what the answer to it might do for you.

•   •   •

*Only in growth, reform, and change
(paradoxically enough) is true security to be found.*

Anne Morrow Lindbergh

I had moved to the community in the country in 1974 and started immediately to look for a new career, or at least a new way to earn a living. Within a few months I started running my "Being in Transition Seminars," and I learned a great deal in doing so, both about what transition does in people's lives and about how to help them to think about and deal with transition in new and more personally enriching ways. Although leading these personal growth groups was extremely valuable to me, I was earning very little money by doing it and I was reaching relatively few people.

As I puzzled over what to do, my old teacher-self kicked in and I found myself thinking that I ought to work for some institution that could promote my work. In that case, I could do what I liked to do, which was to create and conduct learning experiences. (You might be excused if you thought that this was my wish to have a nice old *college* taking care of all the grimy details of my work life again—although I didn't see it that way, of course.)

In 1979, an opportunity came up. A personal growth center—which ran encounter groups, meditation classes, yoga sessions, and a dozen other kinds of activities that were common in the Human Potential Movement of those days—announced that it was looking for a director. What a coincidence, I thought. I was looking for a new venue to do my work, and it was looking for a person like me.

I began to dream: I could turn that growth center into a life-transition center, where people would come to get help with transition when they were changing careers or getting a divorce or just wrestling with midlife issues. We could even send people out on walkabouts and vision quests. We could help them, as the Aesculapian dream-temples helped seekers in the classical world, to find the meaning of the dreams and the other ways that the gods speak to us. I could. . . . well, I won't burden you with all the ideas I had about what I could do in that position. Suffice it to say, I only hoped that they could recognize how *perfect* I was as a candidate.

I shared some of these ideas with the committee that was interviewing candidates for the director's position, and they seemed interested in them. (Or else I overwhelmed them and left them speechless. Afterwards, I wondered which it had been.) One of them said that the other candidates hadn't had any ideas like that—another enigmatic cue that I took to be a positive sign—and I decided that I was a shoo-in. I told my friends about my new role; I even canceled a couple of upcoming events that would clash with my beginning on the date they wanted the new director to take over, and I got ready for the call that would give me the good news. But it didn't come. A couple of days after the announced decision date, I called the head of the search committee and was told that they had chosen another person.

The crashing sound that ensued was the collapse of all my hopes and dreams, not to mention my pride—why in the world had I told my friends all about my new job? It was a big, unexpected, embarrassing ending and a big loss, both to my plans and my self-esteem. I felt very depressed and for a week or so I couldn't do much of anything. But then one day I woke up and found myself thinking that if I was going to be stuck with this empty calendar, I might as well take a shot at writing a book based on the transition groups I had been running. So I wrote *Transitions*.

Now, thirty-seven printings and a quarter of a million copies later, that appears to have been a good idea—the sort of idea that one would like to take credit for. But it was something that I did only because a breakdown of my plans left me with time on my hands. I would never have done it if my dreams hadn't crashed into reality. And if I hadn't done it, I would have taken much longer to let go of my belief that I needed an institution backing me, too. If my plans had worked out, I wouldn't have continued to wrestle with my dark angel about needing to earn a living, for I would have walked right into a small but passable salary. That wrestling proved to be not only a powerful discipline in itself, but it kept me thinking about working-without-a-job until in 1994 I wrote a book about doing that, called *JobShift*.

You could say, in fact, that my big life change in 1974 left me with two questions. The first was "Why is transition so difficult?" And the second was "How do you support yourself without a regular job?" As

I lived with those questions over the following years, quite without intending to, I began a long journey. For I spent the next twenty years of my life creating the answers by living them.

In my last year of teaching literature, I had come across a passage in one of Ralph Waldo Emerson's essays had that stirred me in ways that I did not fully understand at the time. It became a kind of koan to me, a phrase which (if it could be understood) would hold the key to the things that my life was calling me to understand. Now, koans aren't meant to be explained, so let me just end this chapter by quoting it and asking you to let it reverberate inside you. You can also ask yourself what it would say about your own current transition if you took it, as I did, personally.

> Every man's condition is a solution in hieroglyphic to those inquiries which he would make; he lives it as life before he perceives it as truth.[2]

Certainly, I lived out those two issues for a long time before I saw the personal meaning shining through them. Experience is a tough hieroglyphic to crack. But it is true to the original: It *is* the original, for until something makes sense in the context of our experience, it is just hearsay. So let me invite you to leave behind these ideas and return with me now to the original experience from which they came.

four

Letting Go of My Life

And to make an end is to make a beginning.
The end is where we start from.

T. S. Eliot

There is hardly anything that one can say about losing a loved one that isn't so commonplace that it hardly feels worth saying. The days after Mondi's death were both completely empty and utterly full—empty of life and full of activity. Much of the time I sleepwalked through the things I had to do, so numb that I was often completely unaware of what was going on around me. I felt as though, like some latter-day Noah or Pinnochio, I had been swallowed by some immense whale of an experience. There in the darkness, I was cut off from all that I had thought was "my life."

But then a little event or a few spoken words would bring me out of my darkness, and I would find myself standing alone and confused on some strange shore, full of feeling and memories. Many nights I went to bed exhausted, then lay awake for hours. When I closed my eyes, I would see a blur made up of indistinct images, and it was only when I finally fell asleep and began to dream that anything coherent emerged.

In one dream, Mondi and I had been separated and had been on our way to being divorced. In another dream, I hugged her good-bye and we parted, whereupon a nearby woman began to sob. The woman asked me accusingly, "Is *that* all that you're going to do?" In the dream, I realized that she knew that this was not going to be just a temporary parting, so I ran after Mondi to say a real good-bye to her. But I could not find her, and at the end of the dream I was still looking for her.

I found these dreams disquieting and irritating. They made me feel as though I was handling my loss badly. I wondered if they were telling me that I was somehow not *getting it.* And yet at times they were so clear and memorable that I felt as though my daytime life were full of sleep and my nighttime world of dreaming were my waking.

My three daughters and I were working out the details of the memorial service, at the same time that we were notifying friends and family members, putting notices in local papers, and answering the continually ringing telephone. Flowers arrived at the house almost hourly, although with the remodeling project having plunged the house into chaos there was no good place to put them. I ended up with the flowers surrounding me in the study and scattered around the deck outside the door. Through all of the busyness, I felt as though we were all actors in some badly constructed play.

How does the universe run its appointment calendar? Why in the world were we in the midst of remodeling the living room and kitchen when Mondi died? It was a project that we had started several months earlier, when it looked as though she was solidly in remission. Now, that whole area of the house was an empty shell, and I was living where she had died—in a study under the garage.

Whenever I entered what had been our home, I saw in the age-darkened inner walls of studs and boards, the way the house had built up though a succession of additions and remodelings. Right in the middle of the living-room wall was a break that had been hidden behind the Sheetrock and under the flooring—a dividing line between the darker, cruder boards of the original structure and the lighter, more carefully milled boards of a subsequent addition. Six feet inside the front door, there was a break where the house had once ended. High on the wall, in another spot, there were the signs of a fire that must have burned a corner of the living room. It felt precarious living in the midst of so much evidence of life's mutability.

I often thought about the way outer life mirrors inner life. In life as in housing, I was stripped down to the studs. Some outer semblance of order would ultimately be restored—I knew enough about transition to understand that—but for now my house and my life were utterly dismantled. I was fascinated with that state, in a kind of morbid way, however, and I spent hours standing around, doing nothing, in the unlit, dead living room which had once been filled with furniture and voices. The wiring ran here and there along the walls, like some weird nervous system. A previous owner had done a lot of remodeling himself, and the way he patched and spliced and capped and tied things off made me nervous. It worked, but it looked like a catastrophe waiting to happen. The house, like my life, was definitely not up to code.

The remodeling complicated my life in practical ways. Near the end of the project, they discovered that the front steps that came down from the street to the deck were rotting out and had to be replaced. For several weeks, therefore, all traffic to and from the house had to go down or up a ladder that leaned up against a doorway into the side of the garage, eight feet above the deck. I would come home at night to a dark house, feel my way down a ladder, pick my way across an unfinished deck on the supporting timbers, and let myself in to a study that now doubled as a bedroom and a living room. I had talked for years about how you had to take your life to pieces before you built it anew, but this was ridiculous! Or maybe it was poetic justice.

•   •   •

To every thing there is a season, and a
time to every purpose under heaven:

> *. . . A time to weep, and a time to laugh;*
> *a time to mourn, and a time to dance.*
>
> Ecclesiastes 3:1

I thought a lot about Mondi in the days after she died, of course, but it wasn't quite the kind of thinking that I had expected to be doing. I wasn't flooded by warm memories, and I didn't miss her in the way I had missed her in the past when she had been away for a few days. Now her absence was palpable. It was a tangible fact that she wasn't there, and that fact made her emotional presence very powerful. It was less that I had feelings or thoughts about her than that I perceived her *in-absentia*. It was as though there was always nearby, a shape cut out of space, an empty silhouette of nothingness shaped exactly like her.

Whenever I thought about her, I found myself wondering where she was now. We had read *The Tibetan Book of Living and Dying* together, and I tried to recall what it had said about the bardos, those strange states of existence that the Tibetan Buddhists believe a soul goes through after death. What was it like in the bardos? I kept worrying about her—the way I might have worried if she had been gone on some ordinary, but difficult and risky journey. I couldn't get it out of my mind that she might be in trouble.

My worry had nothing to do with a conventional afterlife in which she could be judged or punished. Rather, I imagined her in some new and unfamiliar world in which things made no sense to her. I worried that she was lost and alone and frightened somewhere in this world after death, and didn't know where to turn for help. Those thoughts filled me with a deep sadness, and I wept more when I worried about where and how she was now than I wept over her death, *per se*. When I imagined talking to her, it wasn't to reminisce about our past life together, but to offer her support and encouragement for whatever she was facing now.

Early one morning a few days after she died, I came out of the door of my study-bedroom and climbed the ladder to the street to go for a walk. At the top, just outside the front gate, I found a perfect, long, black crow's feather. Those birds lived noisily in the tall trees below the house, but I had never found one of their feathers before. It lay at my feet, silent and somber, like a dark note that had been left there, just for me. Recalling how she had lain on the bed in the study just ten days earlier and watched those ebony birds outside the window, I picked up the feather and rubbed it against my cheek. Then, not knowing what else to do, I stuck it in the band at the back of the baseball cap that I was wearing—and went for my walk.

I had not slept very well and I felt tired that morning, so I chose a road that I seldom took that curved downhill through the redwoods into a canyon near my home. I hiked along automatically, preoccupied with the dream I had awoken from an hour earlier. In it, Mondi and I had parked our car so that she could go in for an appointment that she had with someone. I waited for her, sitting on the passenger side of the car for a few minutes. When she didn't come back, I moved over into the driver's seat and started the car. I was almost home before I began to worry about leaving her. Would she have expected me to wait for her? I wished that we had made more definite plans about how we would meet. The dream ended with me wandering around our house, wondering whether I ought to drive back to where we had parked but afraid I would miss her if she had already started to walk home by another route.

Lost in speculation about why my dreams seemed so pedestrian— after all, I knew that some people *talked with* their loved ones in their dreams—I walked absentmindedly down the tree-lined street until. . . There on the road in front of me was another crow's feather! I stopped and picked it up. Standing in the cool shade under the trees, I began to shiver. I stuck the second feather under the cap-strap beside the first and started walking again, more rapidly.

What was going on, I wondered? These were big, glossy feathers free of road-dust, as fresh as if they had just dropped from the wing of a passing bird. I had never found such feathers on my walks before. Were they. . . no, that was ridiculous. I must be really desperate for a message from Mondi to think that she was leaving feathers for

me! My mind drifted off into recollections of people who started be-
having strangely under the pressure of bereavement. I found myself
wondering whether I was betraying any other symptoms of coming
undone.

Looking back, what strikes me now is not my strange behavior
or the mystery of where those feathers were coming from, but
rather the way my mind was trying and failing and trying again
and again to re-establish a critical connection that had been broken. At a level far below consciousness, I was trying to become
whole again. Letting go, I saw, is not a simple act of release. It is a
drawn-out process of exploring whether or not a broken connection can be re-established. The psyche operates the way the body
does, when it seeks to reroute blood through other vessels if the
proper pathways are cut or blocked. I had tapped into my psyche's
own auto-dial system that kept trying to get through when the
original call couldn't be completed. We don't let go of anything important until we have exhausted all the possible ways that we might
keep holding on to it.

•   •   •

*You make what seems a simple choice: Choose a man or a job or a
neighborhood—and what you have chosen is not a man or a job
or a neighborhood, but a life.*

Jessamyn West

As the weeks went by, it became clear that what had been cut off
was not just our relationship, but also all the hopes, fears, dreams
and beliefs that had been connected with our relationship. There
were positive ones, like the dream of watching our grandchildren
grow up, and negative ones, like the nagging feeling that I had always
had that (no matter what I did) I could never really prove that I
cared deeply about her. Then there was the belief that we both
shared that she was the person of feeling and that I was essentially a
cool-hearted person.

I had always told my clients that if you let go of only the external (the person and the relationship itself), but didn't let go of the internal associations that had come to cluster around it, you would just find another person or relationship and attach the same hopes, fears, dreams, and beliefs to that one. That way, you would go through a change but not a transition—and you could count on ending up right back where you started.

Over the next few weeks, I kept finding new dimensions to my loss—or "losses," for there turned out to be *so many* ways that her needs and feelings and habits and worries and hopes for the future had been woven into my life. As the numbness of the initial shock wore off, I kept finding new (and yet further new) ways in which I felt stripped and dismantled by her death.

One of my experiences in those first weeks—and I kept experiencing it to a diminishing degree through the ensuing months—was a feeling of being a smaller, lesser, more inconsequential person than I had been when she was alive. Her loss made me feel less substantial, or more naked. I had never recognized until then how she had *amplified* me, reflected me back and made me more believable to myself. That had developed so gradually through our years together that I had never noticed it, but when she was no longer there I suddenly felt—it's hard to put into words—*flimsy*.

The second thing that her death took away from me came from the fact that it was through our marriage that I grew beyond the lonely and isolated young man I had been when we first met. With her death, I lost the way to find—and for a long time, the *only* way I knew how to find—intimacy. My reliance on her to supply my needs of intimacy had sometimes been a painful issue between us, for she often complained that I was—in her psychological jargon—by nature "unrelated." Being my emotional lifeline to the world was a strain on her, she said. The strain was worse because I did not share much of myself with her emotionally.

We were, at the time of her illness, just coming out of a time in which she had talked darkly about having to get her need for intimacy met "in other ways." I had felt threatened by such talk, imagining the other men she might turn to in order to make up for my inadequacy. At the same time, and in spite of feeling threatened, I also believed that in seeing me as unrelated and without feeling, she was not seeing me accurately. I felt misunderstood by her, but the very fact of her talking about the great difficulty I had with intimacy made me feel her death as a terrible moment of truth. It was the loss of what I myself half-believed was the only experience I could ever have of loving someone. So her dying seemed to take away not only our relationship but my very ability to relate deeply to another person. It seemed to take away not only her love, but also my lovability.

It was more than a year after she died that I was able to sort out what were my issues and what were hers in the matter of my being either able to (or worthy of) love. Nor was I until then able to distinguish between the loneliness that I experienced because she was gone, from the more devastating loneliness that I felt because the only person who (I had almost come to believe) could ever love me had died. Since she defined herself as my connection to humankind and to my own heart, losing her felt at first like the fulfillment of all my childhood fantasies about being abandoned and left to fend for myself in a world that was big and frightening. Those fantasies hooked into archetypal fantasies of being expelled from the human contact of the village or the tribe and doomed to wander as an outcast. I found myself thinking in those first months after she died, "This is what an exile feels like."

The outcast loses more than just a place in a society, however. The psychic loss is far greater, for belonging to the tribe provides you with a constant affirmation of how you see and understand things by keeping you together with others who see and understand them in the same way. To the extent that a relationship is characterized by similar assumptions, values, dreams and views, it serves to affirm each of its parties the way a traditional village or a tribe does. In spite of our disagreements and our very considerable differences, Mondi and I got that affirmation from each other.

Even in the areas where we were very different, the difference itself served to bond us by giving us a kind of effective "division of labor":

She took care of emotional issues, while I handled practical ones; she was enthusiastic and excitable, while I was calm and sensible; she remembered the details that made life run smoothly, while I dreamed the dreams that shaped the directions we moved in. So, when she died, I felt as though I had lost my connection to feeling, excitement and a solid grounding in everyday reality.

There were still further losses, although some of them may seem trivial. For example: Mondi was not only my wife. She was also the way in which I could tell if my socks matched, my fly was zipped, my hair was combed, and my tie was straight. At a little deeper level, she was how I knew if I was talking too much, how I could be sure that conversation would begin when we had company, and how I remembered to send presents to our grandchildren. Because she was good at things I wasn't so good at, she enhanced my life and made me feel more whole.

I could go on with these *collateral* or *extended* losses much further, but one more will suffice. In any relationship, the other person is the reason (or at least the excuse) for not doing some things that you think that you might otherwise like to do. The other relationships you do not pursue, the adventuresome-sounding activities or trips you pass up, the professional ventures you do not engage in, the wonderful things that you could buy yourself but don't—each of these unexplored possibilities can be dismissed because your partner would not like them, or simply because your life together cannot accommodate them.

And then the person is gone. Suddenly—although the shock of the loss may hide the fact for a while—your excuse is gone. You *could* go to Nepal next spring; you could take that person out to dinner; you could drop everything and go to the movies; you could. . . do almost anything. And when you realize that, you find that the freedom you longed for is also more frightening that you realized. What you have lost is *the reason I have to be the person that I currently am.* And that is no small loss, if you have any doubts about yourself.

•   •   •

*Through loyalty to the past, our mind refuses to realize that
tomorrow's joy is possible only if today's makes way for it; that
each wave owes the beauty of its line only to the withdrawal of the
receding one.*

André Gide

In the year before Mondi died, I had begun psychotherapy again.
My hope was partly to have an external source of support during this
difficult time, but I also wanted a way to check out my reactions and
impressions. Mondi was going through times of resenting the difficulties I had coming to terms with the seriousness of her illness—
and, at a deeper level, for being so different from her.

She and I went to see *Shine*, the movie about the pianist whose life
had been so terribly warped by his harsh and cruel father. As we
walked out, I said how much the story had moved me. Mondi too
had had a harsh and cruel father, and I had no sooner started to talk
about the character in the film than she grew very upset that I could
be sympathetic with a movie character but unmoved by her own
real-life suffering at the hands of a similar man.

Larry, my psychotherapist, was wonderful. He would listen to me
and sympathize, then talk about Mondi and sympathize with the
pain she must be feeling as she watched her life unraveling in front
of her. I didn't have to apologize to him for not feeling what I wish I
had been feeling, or for thinking of myself at times when a *good person* would have thought of her. Then, after she died, he listened to
my despair or simply sat with me while I found no words to say.

One day, six months after she had died, I found myself explaining
to Larry how I was looking at my situation. I said that in *Transitions*,
which I had written all those years earlier, I had talked about the four
cardinal aspects of the experience of loss:

1. *disengagement,* which was the separation from whatever it is
   that you have lost;
2. *disidentification,* or the way that the loss destroys the old
   identity you had;

3. *disenchantment*, which referred to the way that the loss tears
   you out of the old reality you accepted unthinkingly;
4. *disorientation* was how, as a result of losing the object of
   your feeling and the identity you had together and the reality you shared, you feel bewildered and lost.

I have to admit that I was expressing pride that now, more than
fifteen years later, I could say that my analysis of loss clarified what I
was experiencing. I even talked about how when, at last I managed to
move into the neutral zone I hoped to experience the fifth *dis-*: the
discovery of a new life, a new identity and a new outlook. Warming
up to my subject, I told him that the four negative *dis-* words were
really just the preconditions for discovery, since they cleared the
ground so that the new thing could be found or created.

Larry said that all of that sounded right, but added that he suspected that I might have to deal with another *dis-*word before I encountered any significant new discoveries. "I think you may find
yourself struggling with the issue of *disloyalty*," he said. "The very
idea that something new and meaningful can come out of Mondi's
death may make you wonder if that doesn't mean that you are being
disloyal to her." I said that I'd have to think about that, but I knew
from the discomfort I felt as I left his office that he was right. Over the
next three months I looked for the signs of feeling disloyal, as though
they were the tracks of the snow leopard. I found that, yes, I felt disloyal almost any time I tried something new and interesting. It made
me feel that I must have been very codependent, and I wrestled with
that issue for a while. Then I felt disloyal that it wasn't until she was
gone that I had recognized and dealt with my codependence. Why
hadn't I been able to deal with it when she was alive and our relationship could have benefited from dealing with it? But then I decided
that *that* was codependent thinking, and that my task now was to find
out who I really was without her—and who I wanted to become.

The issue was somewhat abstract at that point. After all, I wasn't
starting some new work activity or a new relationship that had been
made possible by her death. True, I was going to the movies more,
and was going to concerts. She hadn't enjoyed doing these things as

much as I did, and so we didn't do them together as often as I would
have liked—which meant that most of the time we didn't do them *at
all*. When I stopped to think about it, I did have to admit to feeling a
little twinge of disloyalty.

And disloyalty cropped up in another way too. In talking to
friends—even in writing the passage above about her being angry
with me after we saw *Shine*—I could feel a taboo in myself against
saying anything that could be seen as critical of her. But part of what
makes mourning such hard work is that the ties that you had with
the lost one are woven of dark strands as well as light ones. The old
resentments and hurts make mourning the person doubly hard.

Loss was such a complex experience! Layer after layer of meaning.
No wonder that, in dream and memory, mourning sent you back
over the ground again and again. No wonder mourning took so long
to complete and to move beyond. No wonder that people who make
a change without mourning the loss of the past usually find it con-
fronting them later on, down the road. No wonder that it takes more
than a ceremony to lay someone to rest.

·   ·   ·

. . . and unto dust shalt thou return.

Genesis 3:19

Mondi had not wanted to be buried, so that meant there would
not automatically be a place for her survivors to go when they
wanted to remember her. I could store her ashes somewhere, of
course, but you don't visit a shelf or a drawer as you do a grave site.
Until I picked up her ashes from the mortuary where she had been
cremated, I had not really thought about the problem. But when I
did, I realized that having a place was important to me. The place
had to be outdoors and it had to be beautiful. There was no one particular spot that she had especially loved, although she was always
drawn to Mt. Tamalpais, the mountain that rises up steeply behind
the town where we lived.

The weekend after I picked up her ashes, I drove up the mountain. Almost immediately, I felt foolish. I had no idea where I was going. I had left all my hiking maps of the mountain at home, although I also wondered what help they would have been since what I was seeking wasn't a site that you could locate on a map. So I kept driving, believing that somehow I would find the right place and that I'd know it when I found it. I vaguely had in mind a place that we had gone ten years earlier for a friend's outdoor birthday party, but I couldn't now recall which trail we had taken to it. All I remembered was the view, out to the west, over the Pacific.

I had driven almost to the top of the mountain before I had come to a large gravel turnout. Across from it was a lovely slope that faced west. It wasn't the place I had remembered, but it attracted me in the same way. I pulled the car in and crossed the road to a spot where two paths led out through the dry golden grass and across the slope, one curving upward and the other going down. I instinctively chose the lower one and started walking. The mountain tilted up to my right and down to my left, with my chosen path a little ribbon of dirt that curved in and out, over the undulating contours of the slope. I followed it for fifteen minutes, gradually descending until I reached an outcropping of rock that granted a wide view of that part of the mountain.

From the outcropping, I could see below and ahead of me several clusters of live oak trees and a dry stream-bed full of bay trees. As I studied the vista, I found my eye returning again and again to one of the clusters of oaks. It was tucked in a little behind a knoll, and it was anchored at the top by a broken rim of stone. Without knowing why, I felt that this was the spot I was looking for.

I walked down the last several hundred yards of the path that led, steeply down now to the knoll and sat down on one of the rock outcroppings. This is it, I thought to myself. This is *her spot*. She had loved live oak trees, like the ones that had dotted the hills above Palo Alto where she had ridden her horse as a child. There were five such trees in this spot—one for each of us in her family, I thought. So I spoke to her and told her that we had found her a new home.

•   •   •

A [person's] dying is more the survivors' affair than his own.

Thomas Mann

Several weeks later I returned with my three daughters and three of my grandchildren to scatter her ashes in the little grove of oaks. It was a sunny day. Far below us, the sea flashed silver, while overhead big birds climbed up the stairs of wind coming in from the water. In the distance the tiny figure of hikers crept across the hillside. It was just the kind of a day—and the sort of a group—that Mondi would have enjoyed.

Each of the adults scattered some ashes—and nublets of bone too, for the "ashes" contained those too, which made the remains seem much more real. Tristan and Dylan, aged five and six, chased lizards through the sunny rocks and tried to pretend they didn't know what was going on. Tyler, our five-year-old granddaughter, sat by herself under an oak and watched us do what we were doing. A little later, when we had finished, I notice her reaching upward and wiggling her fingers. Then she smiled and lowered her arm. I went over and sat beside her.

"What are you doing?" I asked.

She was silent and seemed embarrassed. Finally she gave a shrug as though the whole thing was just too hard to explain. Finally she said softly, "Waving to Nana. She is up there, over the trees, you know."

•   •   •

He that lacks time to mourn, lacks time to mend.

Shakespeare

In those weeks after she died, I had a whole string of dreams in which she departed from the house or left on a trip. It was as though I were replaying her death again and again in different symbolic forms. My psyche was running over the experience repeatedly, the way you might have to explain what had happened again and again to a young child who had been through a trauma. And as might a child that was having trouble processing the information, the dreams always finished by posing very elementary questions: Had I said good-bye? Was she coming back? Where was she now? Was she all right?

At first I worried that this repeated motif meant that I was stuck, but as the weeks slipped by and I felt the numbness begin to lift and life return, I began to see that with each visit in dream and fantasy to the subject of her disappearance from my life, I untied another strand of our life together. This was the work of mourning, but it wasn't the tearful grieving that I had expected to endure. Instead, it was long, difficult, mundane work. I went to bed every night tired, even when the day had been uneventful. And after a night of this kind of dreaming, I woke up tired each morning. Thirty-seven years together. Such a lot of knots to untie!

I had always confused mourning with grieving,[1] seeing them both as referring to missing the dead person terribly and weeping when you recalled things that you had done together. Some of Mondi's friends experienced that kind of grieving, but for me mourning was different. It was an almost cognitive process, where inwardly and at levels that I could only occasionally glimpse, I was dismantling a whole life structure and relinquishing the outlook that went with it.

Her death removed a whole way of seeing the world. Being without her was like stepping out of your front door one morning and finding that your neighborhood and its underlying landscape had vanished. But *vanished* isn't quite right, because it was still there. But it was as if you could see right through it. . . could see the other side of it, as you might see the messy tangle of threads on the back of an elegant tapestry. My loss had destroyed my image and had left in its place the underlying weave by which the image had been created.

Ever since I had awakened that morning, beside her dead body, I had had a sense of looking through what I used to call "reality." That body next to me was so much like her, but it wasn't *her*. Little Tyler, had come into the room that morning as soon as she heard that her Nana had died during the night. She had climbed up on the bed where Mondi lay and grabbed her shoulder. She shook it roughly. "Nana! Nana!" she shouted. "Wake up! I know you're fooling. Wake up!"

From that morning on, and to an extent that kept increasing as the days passed, I felt like a traveler whose land no longer corresponded to the map he held in his hand. Or else a traveler who had stumbled into one of those white, uncharted areas on old maps. The loneliness that I felt was entirely different from the lack of company that goes by the same name. It was an aloneness that no togetherness could cancel, an aloneness that company felt alien to and intrusive upon.

•   •   •

*Confusion is a word we have invented for
an order which is not yet understood.*

Henry Miller

Remodeling the house *was* a good metaphor for the way that my life was being taken apart—except that with the house there was a design and a work plan. The outcome had been established before they started taking the old structure down, and although the plan might have to be modified from time to time, I could see that we were generally moving toward the image drawn on the paper. With the house project, I could go in and see just what remained to be done to get to that final image that I had had in mind from the start. It went frustratingly slowly, of course, but I could always comfort myself with the picture in my head of what it would look like when it was finished.

With my life situation, on the other hand, there was no design to move toward. Oh, there were little imagined images, fantasies of a trip that I'd take by myself or changes in my work life that would give me more time to do what I wanted—or even a new relationship with a woman that I might form someday. But these were like the little pictures of house features that you clip from magazines, images and ideas, not a the-way-the-house-will-be-when-we-are-finished plan.

I need to change my metaphor: My situation was not so much like dismantling a house in order to remodel it, as it was like burning it down and then standing in the smoky wreckage wondering if you had the energy to rebuild it. I thought of a talk I had given at a Catholic church after the huge Oakland fire that destroyed hundreds of houses. Two hundred families in that parish had lost their homes. It was a talk on transition, and I had had mixed feelings about giving it because I didn't really know what it was like to lose everything.

In fact, the talk went well, for the people seized on the transition model as a way of making sense of their experiences. The one thing they agreed on was that it was especially hard to let go when you don't know what was going to come next. It is as if you had let go of one trapeze at the circus and then discovered that there were not yet any provisions made for sending another trapeze swinging toward you.

But the transition process does not depend on there being a replacement reality waiting in the wings. You are in transition automatically when some part of your life ends. Predetermined outcomes certainly make things easier, but we're in transition with or without them. If they are not there, we have to create the outcomes ourselves. That is one of the tasks in the neutral zone and one of the reasons why the connection between transition and creativity is so important. But that's the neutral zone. I'd get there in time, but at that point in my own transition experience, it lay far ahead.

Clients had often complained about how difficult it was not knowing where things were going, and I had always commiserated. But now it was my turn to struggle with the implications of that fact. I could feel in myself such a strong desire to see the future that I would have settled for almost any outcome, even if it wasn't a very good one. At least then I could have started steering my course, although my only landmark might have been something I hoped to avoid. What was so hard was not-steering— being surrounded by uncertainty, full of uncertainty, weighed down by uncertainty. Although I didn't know how I was going to manage it, I knew that dealing successfully with the transition was going to require me to accept uncertainty as my new reality.

In one of Mondi's updates she wrote that Ram Dass had said to her, "illness and death are not an error. They are one's curriculum." That metaphor, she added, made simply trying to destroy the cancer cells wrong. Instead,

> . . . what I want to do with the next months or years of my life is to learn from them. I am curious. I'm least curious about physical suffering, but I know that's part of the curriculum too. At present it just scares the hell out of me. I'm most curious about what dying is all about. I'm curious if I'll be able to keep my eyes and heart open for whatever comes. . . . Before I sign off, I want to tell you a quote I heard from Elizabeth Howes, a Jungian therapist. These words are hopeful, comforting and disturbing to me:
>
> > God sends the wound.
> > God is the wound.
> > God is wounded.
> > God heals the wound.

Through those long, long months, as we waited for reports to clarify dark places on X-rays and ambiguous rises in test numbers, Mondi kept her eyes and ears open and remained curious. She kept learning.

Later I found great comfort in that fact: If she could do that as her whole life unraveled, I could do it in the midst of my own much more modest losses. I realized that I had to resist the easy ways out offered by both pessimism and optimism. Pessimism sees all value residing in the past. It offers the reactionary escape from uncertainty by saying, "Nothing good lies ahead. Everything of value exists in the way things used to be." Optimism locates all the value in the future and is based on the progressive escape from uncertainty. It says, "I'll be O.K. as soon as I get beyond the way things now are to a better destination I keep telling myself (Yes! Yes! Yes!) lies ahead."

But both optimism and pessimism are escapes. No, maybe it's fairer to say that they are crutches, useful when you are badly hurt but not what you'd really want to use for your life as a whole. As for that often

praised quality, hope, I had to agree with Lord Halifax: "Hope is generally a wrong guide, though it is a very good companion along the way."
The trouble with hope is that it usually involves not so much a willingness to believe that something new will replace the old—which *is* important—as an affirmation that it will be like or better than the old.

·   ·   ·

Great is the art of beginning, but greater the art of ending.

Henry Wadsworth Longfellow

Eight months after Mondi died, I attended a gathering of consultants that got together each year right after New Years at a resort
north of San Diego. The group contained a few people that I knew
and a number of others I had wanted to meet. I was excited. The
meeting began with a kind of warm-up in which we each talked
about ourselves to some one other person. The man who was leading
the group at this point said, ". . . and tell that person the most important thing that you learned in 1997."

I could have faked it or I could have said that in 1997 I had learned
not to fake things, but I did neither. I simply told my partner about
what a hard year it had been, how I was feeling a bit better now, and
how I couldn't begin to say "what I had learned." Then I sat there and
muttered to myself:

"We Americans always want to put a positive spin on things. 'Oh, I
learned *so much* from that experience,' we say. And we like to see our
lives as an educational process in which we improve. Having gone
through the Holocaust and Hiroshima, we may not believe in societal 'progress' any longer; but we like to think that personally, we
are progressing. That's why we see everything as a—ugh, what a
phrase!—'learning experience.'"

I didn't say most of this aloud, although I did tell the group that I
didn't think I had learned anything through what had been the most
difficult experience I had ever been through. But that wasn't quite
true, for although I resented being asked to give a positive spin to a

huge and terrible year, I had to admit that in 1997 I had learned that the most important ability I possessed was the ability to say good-bye to all that you held dear. It was the ability to make an ending; to do those things, and then go on—even though doing that sometimes feels disloyal.

Endings are transformative experiences. As Eliot says in the epigraph to this chapter, they are often where we start from, for the break they represent in our lives initiates a new chapter even as it winds up an old one. What is difficult, of course, is knowing just what is over and what isn't.

That makes me remember a conference where I spoke ten years ago. A company that helped other organizations relocate their personnel to and from overseas assignments had a booth there advertising its services. At the booth, it gave away as advertising little packets of stickers that a person in transit could use to communicate with movers. There were four labels in the packet. They read as follows:

AIR

This was to be used for important things that you would need at the new location immediately.

SEA

This one was for things that you wanted to take along, but that were not so important as to require fast transit.

STORAGE

This sticker was to be used with things that you didn't want to discard, but that you also knew you really didn't want to use just now.

THIS STAYS

This was to be put on things that you realized that it was time to get rid of and leave behind.

If they made such stickers for people in transition, I could certainly have used a package in 1997.

five

The Way of Transition

Age seldom arrives smoothly or quickly. It's more often a succession of jerks.

Jean Rhys

I've always been fascinated by biography. Not big LIFE AND TIMES OF SO-AND-SO tomes, but those little lists of vital dates that outline a lifetime in a page or so—book jackets and obituaries are my specialty. I am always tracing out the pattern as I read: "1945—that means that he was twenty-four when he published that first book." When I was young, the thing that drew me to such lives-in-brief was the question of whether I was on a timetable that would get me anywhere. I remember feeling a great sympathy for comedian Tom Lehrer's crack: "When Keats was my age, he'd been dead for five years!" After a while, of course, he could no longer say that and had to redo his chronology, so it became "When *Mozart* was my age . . ." That worked through Lehrer's thirties, but then the joke died.

Toward the end of my own thirties, while I was still a literature professor at Mills College in Oakland, California, I taught a course in autobiography. I wasn't an expert on that subject. I was just looking for a subject that even students without any confidence could write about with some authority. My idea was that much of the difficulty that many students have writing well begins with the fact that they do not know enough about their subject to write the way good writers must: from their own minds and hearts. (Remember those grammar-school papers that you wrote on China? They told you that you had to footnote everything that you took from a secondary source. Which was *everything*. No one can write well under those conditions.)

So I designed a freshman writing course in which we read several different kinds of autobiographies and some material about the how's and why's of autobiography-writing. All the papers for the course were chapters from the student's own evolving autobiography. It worked well, which is to say that even the students who didn't write very well wrote pretty well when they were describing things about which they were the undoubted expert. And it worked well in the sense that the students discovered that writing about something could be a way of learning about it, for as they viewed their lives from this angle and that, tried describing them in one way and then another, they learned much more about things that they thought they knew everything about when they began the assignment.

Although I started this project with the goal of only improving their writing skills, I soon found that I was seeing in the students' chapters the ways in which they developed in the years before college. A few of my students were what we called in those days "older" students, the patterns of development sometimes covered the adult years as well. As time went on, my secondary interest in the content of what they were writing about began to steal the show from what I was supposed to be focusing upon—the writing itself.

The students found that the very task of breaking their lives into "chapters" was a valuable exercise.

Let's see—is Chapter One birth-to-five, because those were the years we lived in Boston, or do I do birth-to-three, because when Bobby was born (I was three), I was no longer an only child? And do I start with my own birth, or do I start with a chapter about my parents. . . or grandparents, who immigrated from Ireland just after World War I? Or, maybe I have to start with me as an adult, finding those letters in my grandmother's closet two years ago.

And the question of how to organize the chapters kept students awake at night, even though the abstract question of how humans develop hardly mattered to most of them at all, except when it threw some light on their autobiographical venture. I remember one student puzzling for days over the phrase, *The End of Childhood*. Another wrote a very thoughtful essay on the way that discovering reality under the surface appearance of normality in her extremely unhappy and neurotic family was an enormous step forward in her own development.

Again and again, the students described significant transitions as the turning points in their lives. Not changes, but transitions. I think that this was when I first became aware of the difference between the two. The *change* might have been a geographical move or the graduation from high school or the breakup of their parents' marriage. The *transition* was the way that that student's life took a turn, and was different after that point. Looking back, they usually felt that the changes were simply the trigger and the marker for their transitions.

I started wondering: Why had the transition happened when it did? And how could an apparently small change trigger off a big transition? Why were some students vulnerable to changes at school, while others were shaped by family changes? And why did transitions so often "snowball" at particular points in a lifetime, so that several were packed into a short span of time?

Soon I found myself reading everything I could find on adolescent and early-adult development. When I had gone to college, human development was *child* development. Even in 1970, when I was teaching the course, those step-style diagrams which illustrated the stages of development showed early childhood, the school years, adolescence and young adulthood as a stairway mounting toward adulthood proper. Then they opened out on the adult plateau where. . . where you just "lived," with development behind you. Transitions did not stop in adulthood—I could attest to that. But perhaps they no longer had a developmental component to them. It seemed to me that they did, however.

There were a few articles out there on something called "adult development"—an extension of the stair-steps through to the period that was coming to be called *mid-life*. Gail Sheehy hadn't yet raised that subject up to public awareness with her book, *Passages,* but there was enough in print then to make it clear that other cultures had given people a much more extensive map of their lifetimes than our culture had. Confucius, for example, had written,

> At fifteen I set my heart upon learning.
> At thirty I established myself.
> At forty I no longer had perplexities.
> At fifty I knew the mandate of heaven.
> At sixty I was at ease with whatever I heard.
> At seventy I could follow my heart's desire without transgressing
> The boundaries of right.[1]

I envied people who could chart their course by such a clear guide. Since I was nearly forty and very confused myself, I read the line about being without "perplexities" with great envy.

In the developmental timetables laid out by traditional figures and modern researchers, the times of transition tended to disappear. Like stairways on a house plan, they were simply how you got from one level to the next, not living spaces themselves. But my students thought otherwise. For them, the transitions were the real thing, the important times. The periods of relative stability before and after the transitions were times when they could catch their breath and move forward without whatever they had put behind them. These were times of consolidating whatever had come into their lives during the last transitions.

To my students, it was the story of their transitions, not the stages of living that they had moved through, that told them how they had come to be the people they were. Transition was the force that moved them forward along whatever path they were following. It was the dynamic of life itself.

Not every change in their lives created significant transitions, of course, although that fact itself was perplexing. Some of my students went through huge upheavals in their life situations without missing a beat personally. On the other hand, changes that most people would have considered little ones—the death of the family dog, making a new friend, or taking a vacation on which they had a first, minor romantic experience—were the triggers for enormous inner redirections and realignments which left them very different people than they were before. These shifts were triggered by changes, but they resulted from some inner developmental force with a life of its own. So I came to agree with the students, that life could be seen as a journey in which the transitions were the traveling part and the so-called stages were simply the stopovers.

As I began to see things that way, I realized that throughout nature development is episodic. That fact is recorded in a tree's rings on the cross-section of its trunk. It also shows up in the way that a human baby changes very slowly over a period of months and then in only a few days gets to its feet and begins to take steps—in the way that it babbles for weeks and weeks, and then in a few days begins to speak recognizable phrases. The same fact is obvious in the way that water gets colder, degree by degree, without changing its physical form, until it gets down to 32° Fahrenheit, where suddenly crystals start to form; in a matter of minutes, if the temperature falls just a little more, the liquid will turn into a solid chunk of ice.

• • •

When things reach maturity, they decay of themselves.

Lao-tzu

With human beings, transitions leave in their wake not only people who are different in some way. Transitions also make the world look significantly different to those people. Letting go of a fantasy about family solidarity after your parents divorce or letting go of a view that others are asexual after your first sexual experience doesn't just make you a different person. It redefines *reality*.

In tribal societies, there were rites of passage to serve as vehicles to carry people across the gap between one life phase and the next.

These ceremonies not only gave young people a new identity in the tribe, but also introduced them to a new and adult view of the world. The young people might be allowed to see "backstage" at a tribal ritual, and understand thereby how the magic of the event was produced. Or they might be introduced to secret knowledge about a sacred spot near the village. Whatever the new insight, it was usually preceded by a kind of ritual disenchantment by which the old reality, appropriate to the younger person, was destroyed so that they could see the world through adult eyes.[2]

That there are no official disenchantments in our society doesn't mean that there aren't dozens of unofficial ones during the life-journey. Nor does it mean that these times of accelerated development and sudden awakening to something beyond what one used to understand aren't still an important part of growing up. It was, in fact, as I read my students' accounts of their early disenchantments that it first occurred to me that life-transitions might be most meaningfully understood as unritualized points of *passage*, very much like the ones that tribes celebrate ritually.

Underneath all tribal passage ritual was a view that there are really a succession of worlds, like those little, wooden Russian dolls, where each one has another nested inside it. The disappearance of an official version of the reality sequence does not mean that reality no longer "develops" as a person grows older. All that it means is that we no longer have an effective way to prepare people for the likelihood that what we take to be "the world" can vanish in a moment of transition. Nor do we have good ways to help them through that experience.

We lack an official recognition of the truth that, in the words of English playwright Christopher Fry, "there will always be another reality to make fiction of the truth we think we've arrived at."[3] If a transition goes satisfactorily, of course, it finishes with a new pattern of meaning emerging from the chaos left by the destruction of the old one. But since we lack the societal acknowledgment of (and any social support during) most of these disenchantments, the experience easily degenerates into simply one of personal loss. In that case, it is stripped of its significance. The person in such a transition is no longer someone shedding an outlived shell of reality, but simply a victim of an unfortunate (and essentially meaningless) personal experience.

Yet disenchantment is built right into human development, just as withering and decay are built into nature. Each of us lives in a world, and that world is meant to dry up in its time like a withering flower to make way for the growth that follows it. Lacking an understanding of the process, we are depressed and discouraged when it happens. We say that things aren't going well for us. We look for ways to solve our problems, fix things, and get our lives back on track again. Of course, "back on track" means "back on the track they were on before we encountered this difficulty." And that means "back into the life that it was actually time to let go of."

Now, I am not claiming that our lives never need repair or that every difficulty is a sign that developmental disenchantment is at hand. I am just saying that our active-minded, mechanistic culture is highly alert to the need to *fix things* and very oblivious to the way that problematical life situations can serve as signals to alert us to an imminent transition. Most of us have been raised to define courage as the emotional fortitude that enables us to hold fast during difficult times, when the courage that is often called for is the courage to let go. In our culture we are encouraged to seek out advice about what we should *do*, when *doing nothing* but listening and watching for transition-related signals may be the best way to move forward through our difficulties.

• • •

Life is the only real counselor.

Edith Wharton

The temptation to look for ways to protect the life we already have is especially strong in the middle years, when so much seems to depend on the position and the identity that we have established by the activities we're engaged in and the roles we fill. At such a time, we are like the mythical figure of Odysseus who spends his whole trip back from the Trojan War getting one signal after another that he must find a new way to handle adversity. His difficulties reach their climax when he tries to squeeze his ship between the six-headed monster, Scylla, and the whirlpool, Charybdis. The sorceress, Circe, had told him that he would be able to get through this narrow space between the archetypal rock-and-a-hard-place only by *not taking action* against the threat that they posed. When he finally reached the narrows, however, he fell back on his old reality and the behavior that had been appropriate to it:

> And then I forgot the hard injunction of Circe
> When she ordered me in no way to arm myself.
> I put on my famous armor, took two long spears
> In my hands, and went up on the deck of the ship
> At the prow.[4]

Like most of us, in the crunch he fell back on what had got him there. He failed to see and treat the problem that life was presenting him with as a signal and a gift rather than a difficulty to be overcome, and so his ship was destroyed.

In the West, we associate development with learning and adding to what is already there—as I realized at my meeting of consultants during the winter after Mondi died. But there is an older (and, I believe, deeper) wisdom that tells us that it is by *unlearning* and stripping away what is there that we grow.

We lack institutions which are based on a pedagogy and offer a curriculum of un-learning. The educational programs that are available emphasize learning, not unlearning. And the religious and therapeutic centers, where such things might happen, all have their dogma which the initiate is meant to learn. Where can we go to dis-identify with all that got us as far as we have gone in life?

Yet life runs a perfect curriculum, and the tuition is modest. If you miss the offerings this year, you can catch them next year. Again and again, it offers us a correspondence course in letting go: Introductory Letting Go, Intermediate Letting Go and Advanced Letting Go. Life does so not because what we are identifying with is bad, but because we are ready for something else, something further, something in some way deeper.

The alternation of letting go of an old world and beginning a new one is the rhythmic pattern underlying life itself. The heart is nothing more than an organ that does that with our blood. Our lungs do the same thing with the air that we breathe. The air does the same thing with blood—leaving it behind when we exhale and reentering it again when we inhale. The earth lets the fallen rain go back into the atmosphere and then reincorporates it after it falls again. The ancient wisdom from Ecclesiastes that tells us that there is a time for living and dying is an affirmation of this basic alternating current of the universe that drives the blood and the breath and the weather, although we sometimes imagine that it is a precursor of modern relativism.[5]

East and West have traditionally taken opposite positions in relation to this cycle. Eastern religions have traditionally embraced the letting-go that characterizes the ending aspect of the cycle, and they have developed sophisticated ways of helping people to break free of the identifications that they have made with the particular reality that they are experiencing. Western thought, on the other hand, has tried to get the most out of the other aspect of the cycle—the identifications, the embodiments, the actualizations that are associated with the transition phase of beginning again in a new cycle.

The problem is, of course, that neither tradition views the two tactics as simply the half-truth components of a cycle. In the West we see "whatever is" as a thing with a beginning, a middle and an end—in that order. The West believes in beginning, and believes further that if you play your cards right that you can hold off an ending for a long, long time. (Shakespeare was very Western when he wrote, "The coward dies a thousand times before his death./The brave man dies just once.") This approach makes an ending into a breakdown and even a failure. The "middle" that comes between the beginning and the ending is what Westerners want to continue as long as possible, and that is why we are so dismayed when we start getting signals that an ending is at hand.

To be fair, the East has its own one-sidedness too. It identifies with letting go and ending, and all the things that are produced by beginnings are dismissed as illusion. The letting go is no longer a dynamic process but a state of detachment that is meant to continue as long as possible, and then recovered if it is lost. What is held onto is very different, but in its way the East is as unwilling to let go as the West: unwilling to let go of letting go.

Both the East and the West believe in a universal energy that might be called DC (direct current), for it is meant to flow in a single direction—a different direction in each case, but a single direction all the same. I am arguing, in contrast, that human beings are AC appliances that operate on a current where the energy "alternates" between ending and beginning, and where stopping at either pole is dangerous.

The pattern of experience and of nature that alternates endings and beginnings results in a kind of a *fishtailing* movement, an undulation between letting go and taking hold again in which each is affirmed in its time and in which the movement between them, like the back and forth sweep of a fish's tail, is the force that carries us forward in our lives. It is the readiness to go back into transition again when the old reality is wearing out that provides us with the force that propels us through life.

When we say that "pride goeth before the fall," we give it a moralistic twist so that it means that we were cast down (bad, bad!) because we were proud. But in the context of the alternating current of development, it simply means that when we reach the apex of existence, where our lives are well in order and fully formed, the transition half of the cycle begins. Pride isn't the cause of our fall, just the timing of it.

And when we find ourselves in transition, we think that we'd better do a little planning. Set some goals. Make a to-do list. Tape up some affirmations on the bathroom mirror. Then when things start to improve, we say that our technique *worked.* We fail to see that we have just come through a long neutral zone and made (at last!) a new beginning. The Greeks thought that such thinking was taking credit for the actions of the Gods, and they called it "hubris." If we are to credit anything for the recovery, it should be life's own built-in AC.

•   •   •

I began to have an idea of my life, not as the slow shaping of achievement to fit my preconceived purposes, but as the gradual discovery and growth of a purpose which I did not know.

Joanna Field

The transition process ends the old and begins the new. Between ending and beginning is the emptiness of the neutral zone, the chaos from which all new life flows. Without the neutral zone, there would be no rebirth. Transition is only one half of the circle, of course, while the world of existence is the other half. Between the beginning that finishes one transition and the ending that starts the next one is the "middle" that is the world. The alternating current of existence takes us into and out of a succession of worlds and realities, a succession that moves toward higher form.

All of this may seem a little removed from our starting point, which was the way that human development is the context within which transition is meaningful. But it is precisely the alternating current generated by transition that keeps us moving down the developmental path toward becoming the unique individual each of us essentially is.

Development is an interesting word derived from a linguistic root meaning "rolled" or "folded." An *envelope* is a folded sheet of paper, and to *develop* is to "unroll" something that has been heretofore so tightly rolled that we could not see what it really was. After the child has grown up, we can say that she was *that way* from the very start. But when she was a child, it was anyone's guess how she would turn out.

The particular individual is an entity that is both utterly unique and profoundly like others. In this paradox of sameness and difference, we are like leaves on a tree or waves on the ocean. This *development* continues up to (and perhaps even beyond) the moment of death, the point at which a one-of-a-kind life dies, which is what every other living thing before it has done.

The path of development is the fishtailing course we follow as we let go of what we have been and then discover a new thing to become— only to let go of that in time and become something new. This is the *Way of Transition*, the way or path of life itself, the alternating current of embodiment and disengagement, expansion and contraction. The word *way* has two meanings: The one we have just used means a path or a route ("We took the long way home."); the other *way* refers to a technique or method ("There is a better way to do that.").

As I speak of the way-as-path, I know that today many people are far more interested in finding a new way in the second sense. They are seeking a new way to lose weight, a new way to raise their child or a new way to improve their marriage. And they would like a new way to deal with transition, too. Well, there *are* some techniques that you can use to deal successfully with transition, and a number of them were described in my earlier book, *Transitions*. And at the end of the present chapter of this book, I describe three techniques that many people have found useful.

But taken by themselves even the best techniques are empty and mechanical approaches to the question of living. The problem with them is the one that French cook Simone [Simca] Beck, referred to in a class where a student kept asking her about the right technique for everything—especially, trivial questions about the right way to measure ingredients. Frances Mayes reports that when the student "asked one time too many, Simca said crisply, 'There *is* no technique, there is just the way we do it. Now, are we going to *measure* or are we going to *cook*?'"[6]

That is the question that must be asked in regard to the elaborate programs offered by the thousands of self-help books flooding the market: Do you want to practice *techniques* or do you want to *live*?

Because life is not reducible to a collection of techniques; and no body of techniques ever added up to—or gave their practitioner—a "life." To me, the wonderful phrase "Get a life!" is not a request to learn anything—just to live, to stop fixating on the right answer, to find your own path and take off.

The way of life is a journey, a journey along a winding path. "All rising to great place," wrote Francis Bacon, "is by a winding stair."[7] Cause and effect, input and output, force and impact: The mechanistic world is made up of "shortest distances," straight lines on a flat surface. But life fishtails its way across an undulating landscape. If you want to *live*, you need to give yourself over to the way of transition—to let go when life presents you with a time of ending, to abandon yourself to the neutral zone when that is where you find yourself, to seize the opportunity to make a new beginning when that moment presents itself.

• • •

How many cares one loses when one decides
not to be something, but to be someone.
Coco Chanel

It is when we are in transition that we are most completely alive. I have often asked groups of individuals that I am working with to introduce themselves, one to another, referring only to those things *that are not changing* in their lives. The result is a soft murmur of voices talking about where they live and how many children they have and what kind of work they do. After everyone has had a few minutes of that, I ask them to reintroduce themselves to each other, speaking this time only of the things *that are changing* in their lives. There is usually a moment of nervous laughter, then a little pause, then there is a wave of talk about the gains and losses that they are experiencing. Before a minute has passed, voices are rising and falling. Intonations are full of energy. There is laughter. Hands are moving in gesture.

Without fail, the second introduction is far more alive than the first—even though it is by *what is not changing in our lives* that we customarily define ourselves or are defined by the academics who want to describe us in terms of the categories we fall into. If you asked the people who had done the two introductions, most of them would say that they are tired of things changing all the time and that they wish that their lives would settle down. Yet it is when they talk about all the changes that they are most animated and energized.

Actually, it is not the fact of being in transition that most people mind, but rather that they cannot place their experience of being in transition within any larger, meaningful context. Without such a context, the endings are for no reason, the beginnings open the door to nowhere, and the neutral zones extend end-to-end across an empty landscape.

The old prescriptive models of life stages—whether from Confucius or from modern psychology—simply fail to match the experience of most modern people. Something is needed that is less rigid and closer to individual experience than theories are. It has to be something that a person can look at and say, "That's it. That's my life." I don't believe that there is any one pattern that fills the bill. So let me suggest three of them. These are not formal "when-you-turn-thirty-eight-you-become-X" patterns. They are more like evocative images, lenses through which you can see and understand your life in new ways. They are:

1. The Chapter Exercise;
2. The Path You Have Followed;
3. The River Named "You."

•   •   •

You may want to pause in your reading through the book now and spend some time on these three exercises. Try on each of these three metaphors as a possible context for the transitions you have been through and the one that you may be in now. Or you may wish to continue your reading—going through each of these exercises mentally in the few minutes it takes you to read them—and then return to do them in depth at the end of the book. Either way will work fine, but one way or the other, give them all a try.

The Chapter Exercise

Imagine that you are writing your autobiography. That is not, incidentally, a silly idea. Whenever people come to the point of letting go of anything significant, they naturally get reflective and begin to look back at the path that brought them to this point. That is one reason old people, who are approaching the ultimate letting-go point, so often spend what seems like an inordinate amount of time talking about the past. It is almost as though even the prospect of letting go makes the past more meaningful to them. While we are on it, the route we are following seems twisted and hopelessly indirect, but looking back from the vantage point of wherever it has led, the curves straighten out and an overall direction is more evident.

You could, as I say, write the story of your life now, and you would probably find doing so to be a very interesting, perhaps exciting, and certainly a helpful thing to do. But that is something to undertake later. For now, I want you simply to create the Table of Contents that will appear at the front of the autobiography you will write someday. That means that you have to come up with the chapter titles to your life story. If those chapters are to be grouped into sections, you need to do that—and come up with names for the sections. In choosing titles, go for words and phrases that capture the spirit of that time in your life. "Gasping for Air" or "On Top of the World" or "My Life as a Goldfish" are better than "New York City, 1976–1980."

As you come up with your chapter titles, there are several more general questions that you will have to deal with. One is, how many chapters does your life have? The answer may have something to do with how long you have lived, but you would be surprised how many chapters a meticulous nineteen-year-old can come up with—or how a seventy-year-old can squeeze a whole lifetime into four or five big bundles.

There is no right number, of course, but you shouldn't have so many that you lose your sense of the natural clumps in a mass of individual trees, or so few that you can no longer trace clearly the important turnings in your life path. Whatever you decide the right number is and whether (or not) to cluster them into Parts I, II, and so forth, the form should do justice to the important life-transitions you have been through, the "worlds" you have lived in, the identities you have embraced, and the realities you have experienced. *If you are going to do the Chapter Exercise now, this is the point at which to do so.*

The Path You Have Followed

There are things that you can understand about your life when it is laid out visually in space that are very hard to see when it is abstracted into words. So I'm going to suggest that you draw a large—that means at least as big as 2' x 3' (four such pages taped into a 4' x 6' rectangle would be even better)—a large map of the journey you have followed through life thus far. Use crayons or colored felt-tip pens to do this, both to make the lines heavier and so that you can use colors to convey some of what you want to say. This map can contain a great deal more information than your chapter titles could, and you can suggest things visually that you would have trouble putting into so many words.

- Crossroads where you faced a big decision and made a significant choice
- Side roads that were attractive, but that you didn't let yourself explore
- Sharp curves where you changed your direction completely (Were you steering around an obstacle, or did you suddenly discover a new destination?)
- Places where you found yourself back where you started or dead ends where you had to retrace your route
- Significant mileposts
- Stopover points—for rest, for fun or for. . . what?
- The sites of wonderful experiences ("points of interest," they're called on the highway)

- Destinations you were headed for—before you decided to bypass them and just keep going
- Swamps and deserts
- Washouts, detours and roadblocks
- Steep grades where it was really hard to make it, or downhill stretches where you had to ride the brakes to keep from wiping out
- Places where you broke down, ran off the road or had a collision with someone else
- There are places—natural spots and communities all along your route with names (Name some of the places on your path)

This exercise should be fun. The idea isn't to be "artistic," so don't get preoccupied with how your map looks. Just use the chance to communicate visually, to discover and represent some things about your life that wouldn't come across in the chapters you just did in the previous exercise.

The River Named "You"

The map you have just made is one way of depicting your life-journey. Because you travel actively on a road (on foot, by car, on a bicycle, with others in a bus—how did you envision it?), making choices at crossroads and choosing to speed up or slow down, the road-image emphasizes the traveler as the agent of his or her own journey.

But there is another way of looking at your life. You can think of the course of your life as a river. This time the idea is not that you are a traveler negotiating the river, but that *you are the river*. That opens up some interesting questions.

- Where are your headwaters? Where do you come from? What is your *source*?
- Sources are important to rivers—especially symbolically—but most of the water in them comes from "in-fluence" (or in-flows or tributaries). What are the important in-flows into your life?

- The river gathers its water from a "watershed." What is the country that your life drains? Is it mountainous or are you a river of the plains? Is it populous or is it wilderness?
- Are you wide, shallow, narrow, deep, slow, fast? Are you full of rapids, or do you come down gradually? Or is your course punctuated by heart-stopping waterfalls?
- Are there significant communities along your banks? What are the main things produced in the fields and towns that border your river? What are the exports (and imports) of your river basin?
- Is there much traffic on your river—and what kind? Or are you a white-water river?
- If the source is your origin, the sea is your end and ultimate destination. Where are you presently on your journey to the sea?
- What is the topography of the land that you run through? Rivers encounter mountains and turn; they run into the sands of the desert and nearly dry up; they enter swamps and they split into hundreds of little channels; they even go underground for a time and then reappear later. How is your course shaped by the geography that you run through?

Again, you will discover what you want to portray as you draw it, so these questions are simply meant to get you thinking metaphorically. Take your time and let the river draw itself. This is a discovery process, not a report.

• • •

Whether or not you did these three exercises in depth, they will have offered you different ways of thinking about the path of your own life. Let me supplement them with a couple of questions.

ONE: Choose any point in your past where you went through a significant transition. It may appear in one or more of the exercises, or it may simply be one that you think of when I ask, *When in the past were you really in transition?* Looking back at that time, with the benefits of hindsight and subsequent growth, answer these questions:

1. If that part of your life had been a course in the school of life that you were taking, what could it have been called? What subject were you dealing with in and through that transition?

2. What was it that you needed to *unlearn* for that course? What, in other words, was it time to let go of—not an external thing, but a part of yourself (a habit, an outlook, a goal, a value) or a piece of your reality?

3. To the extent that you did let go and unlearn something and to the extent that you were able to live through the subsequent neutral zone, what new chapter was waiting in the wings of your life, to make an entrance at that point?

The answers to these questions will be interesting and useful to you, but I am asking them at this point not so much for their own sake as to give you a little practice with a situation that is far enough behind you to give you some perspective. Even if you didn't entirely let go of the things that life was then inviting you to let go of back then, you should be able to see now what they were. Which brings us to my second question.

TWO: What is it that your life is calling upon you to deal with at this moment? Take a little time right now, before you go on, and think about your own present transitionality. You may have given your present situation an actual title in the chapter exercise. If you did not, turn back to that exercise and think for a few moments now about what title you would give to the present chapter of your life. Then answer the following questions:

• If the *present* chapter of your life is a course you are taking, what would an appropriate title for it be? What are you meant to be learning in it?

- What is it that you need to unlearn for this course? What is it time for you to let go of? What—or even what chapter of your life—is over *now*?

- Presuming that you can let go and unlearn something and to the extent that you are able to live through the subsequent neutral zone with awareness, what do you think is *now* waiting in the wings of your life to enter? What unlived life is *now* there in the shadows? You may decide not to live it out—that is a whole other question—but it would be a shame not to know that it is there.

These questions are certainly worth a little time right now. You might deal with them better if you could take a little time away by yourself to mull them over.

● ● ●

In some *area of my life, I guess that I am* always *in transition.*

A participant in a "Managing Transition" seminar

So far, we have been speaking as though your whole life goes into transition at one time. But it would be truer to say that any life is made up of many different strands, which start and stop independently of one another. Things hum along smoothly at work, while at home you are trying to come to terms with the arrival of your second child. You are in transition financially, since your house purchase has forced you to let go of the level of security you had grown accustomed to. With the new medication you are taking, your blood pressure is finally stabilized and you feel that your health is once again on solid ground. But psychologically. . . . While some transitions affect your whole life, others have a more limited impact. And you could write a book called "The Story of My Transitions" in any one of a dozen life areas.

The fact that many transitions are limited in scope is fortunate, because it allows you to change your standpoint without losing your footing. As rock climbers try to move only one hand (or one foot) at a time, keeping the other three points of contact with the rock solid, so the person in transition will usually do well to use the rest of his or her life as a series of "holds" while making a transition elsewhere. When that is not possible, however, you feel that "everything is up in the air" and that chaos reigns in your life.

Here's another possibility to consider: For many people, there is some particular area that seems to keep turning up at most of the big transitional points in their lives. Its appearance creates a *theme*. One person's life is essentially the story of his or her relationships. Another's is a career story, and still another's is a spiritual search. What about you? What is the theme of your life?

six

My Intensive Course in Love

"You are not at all like my rose," [said the Little Prince to some roses] ". . . As yet you are nothing. No one has tamed you, and you have tamed no one. You are like my fox when I first knew him. He was only a fox like a hundred thousand other foxes. But I have made him my friend, and now he is unique in all the world. . . . You are beautiful, but you are empty. . . . One could not die for you. To be sure, an ordinary passerby would think that my rose looked just like you—the rose that belongs to me. But in herself alone she is more important than all the hundreds of you other roses; because it is she that I have watered; because it is she that I have put under the glass globe; because it is she I have sheltered behind the screen; because it is for her that I have killed the caterpillars . . . .because it is she that I have listened to when she grumbled or boasted, or even sometimes when she said nothing. Because she is my rose."

Antoine de Saint-Exupéry, *The Little Prince*

In focusing on the last year of our life together, I may have left the impression that Mondi's and my marriage was a rich and rewarding one. But the intimacy of that last year grew out of soil that was rich and deep not only from happy years together but also from the decay of our countless fallen hopes. Each of us had had expectations of the other that had been deeply disappointed. Several times in the course of our thirty-seven years together, one or the other of us had decided that we had gone as far together as we could go. There were many times when not much more than our insecurities held us together. That fact made our leave-taking more complicated than it would have been if there had not been so many dark strands in our relationship.

In spite of our difficulties, for good reasons and bad we stayed married for thirty-seven years, and I am grateful that we did. I am grateful, too, that Mondi lived long enough for me to let go, finally, of my image of myself as a poor guy married to a woman who didn't understand or accept him. Coming to see her as a lonely woman who had been badly damaged by a truly hurtful childhood, not only helped me to lay to rest some of my suspicions about her; it also in the end made her very dear to me and enabled me to take the final steps of her journey by her side. But all of that notwithstanding, I have to say that our relationship was often a difficult and painful one for both of us.

We were an unlikely pair from the start. I came from a traditional New England home, where everyone talked about ideas and no one mentioned money. Mondi came from a California home where money was flaunted, except when her father worried that his children had developed bad values and canceled all the financial promises that he had made to them—and then denied that the promises had ever been made. The only ideas she grew up around were the ones that her father proclaimed in his interminable dinner-table monologues.

I had done practically no serious dating when we met, whereas Mondi had had a string of boyfriends, including several who had asked her to marry them. My mother, who had recently been widowed, lived in a small Maine mill town, in the house where she and several generations before her had been born. Mondi's father, though he had grown up in a room in his family's little oil-workers' hotel in Bakersfield, California, had become a world-famous architect. Just before I came on the scene, he had bought a castle in the Tyrol and was in the process of remaking himself into an Austrian-American "aristocrat."

I was stiff and rationalistic, introverted and shy, an intellectual— but one who had never entertained a really controversial idea. She was an extroverted, energetic and charismatic young woman with a secret core of grief and darkness. I was steady, and everyone knew that I would "go somewhere." When people speculated at what I'd become, they usually pegged me as the one-day dean (or even president) of some small college. When people thought of where Mondi would end up, they imagined her marrying some powerful man. We were birds of a different feather, a strange pair to nest together.

•   •   •

Marriage is our last, best chance to grow up.

Joseph Barth

Marriage is such an unlikely institution. I was sitting at a traffic light the other day, behind a car driven by a woman who was taking that particular pause in her journey as an opportunity to fluff out her hair. It was a complicated process. She had one of those huge, kinky hairdos and her arms twirled above her head as though she were doing some kind of highly kinesthetic movement-therapy, barely missing the head of her husband who sat in the passenger seat next to her. He stared ahead unflinchingly through it all, apparently oblivious to the possibility that his temple could be caved in at any moment by one of her elbows, or that the long rat-tail comb in her right hand might be driven like a spike through his ear and into his brain.

A perfect image, I thought to myself, for the couple who have learned to do all that they need to do in close proximity to each other without inflicting unnecessary damage. And also a good image of the pair who go through the motions, but make no real contact. Early in our marriage, after a flurry of newly married activity, Mondi and I settled into something not so different from the couple at the stoplight.

We had three babies, but they represented changes that did not cause us to make transitions. We were a Hansel and Gretel, who had been captured by the ethos of domestic life. I was especially trapped—it was Hansel who was shut up in the oven, after all—and I might be there still if it had not been for my resourceful Gretel. It wasn't that she knew what she was doing. It was just that she grew bored and decided to take an adult-education course at a nearby university in American Civilization, the field in which I had received my doctorate.

Later she told me that she had taken the course in the naïve hope that it would give her a glimpse of the kinds of ideas that I thought about all day and would, thereby, enable us to talk about interesting things in the evening. What we actually started talking about was a little different, however, although she found it very interesting: It was why we didn't talk more. The course she took, it seemed, was all about relationships in America. The professor was the son-in-law of Carl Rogers, the well-known psychotherapist, and he assigned the class his father-in-law's *On Becoming a Person* as a textbook. Within a matter of hours, she told me she had a book she wanted me to read.

I asked her to give me a one-minute synopsis of the book and then (ten minutes later when I managed to slow her down briefly) told her that the book didn't sound like something I'd be interested in. Well! Wasn't that exactly what she'd imagine I would say! And didn't that show how little I knew about. . . relationships! Starting that day with the subject of why we didn't talk more, we began to talk more.

Not counting the initial adjustments we had made to being married, this barrage of communication represented the first of the huge transitions that we made as a couple. I held out as long as I could and much longer than I should have. Considerably after the situation suggested that I ought to have let go of my stiff, rationalistic (not to say conventional and petty) objections to the transition she was inviting me to make, I finally did let go, and immediately I found myself wandering through a howling neutral-zone wilderness. I, who had never lost an argument since we were married, could now, with no difficulty, lose three before breakfast. I felt completely confused. She, on the other hand, seemed to have come into her own. Although she had briefly emigrated early in our marriage into my world of restraint and understatement, she now found herself back on her home territory: feelings, conflict, passion, intuition.

And I had left my native land, as one often does in the large transitions during early adulthood, when you are exploring different ways of living your life. I read new books, accompanied her to marriage counseling and went to my first encounter group. I also started going to hear talks by social, intellectual, and political reformers. But mostly, I talked with her. I, who had been brought up to live on the principle of parallel-play, found myself nose to nose with this person I was married to. And the changes radiated out from our relationship into every area of my life. I began to experiment with new ways of teaching and began to develop ideas that my New England family hoped that I would get over soon.

In one sense, our marriage stayed fairly stable through all of this external turmoil, but in another sense it began to lose its shape. And although I gained a great deal as I let down the barriers to new ideas and experiences, I also felt as though I were living on quicksand. For the next ten years, she effectively took charge of how we would live and how our marriage would function. On our good days, it felt exciting to be joining her on her journey; on our bad days, it felt as though she were trying to turn me into someone I wasn't. On our good days, she had vast charisma; on our bad days, she was an emotional steamroller.

She never saw herself as powerful, however. As the product of a really abusive family, she had grown up being victimized, and that shaped her self-image in ways that she hardly questioned until she was dying. The "cancer-victim" finally outgrew victimization. Sadly, she didn't have long to enjoy her hard-won victory. For most of her fifty-seven years she experienced herself as someone who was always being hurt: first by an overbearing father, then by men in general, and finally by everyone who did not see how vulnerable she was under the surface.

People always saw and treated her as though she were strong—because, of course, that was how she came across. But she always viewed herself as fragile, because that was how she felt. And so people's misunderstanding of her was a constant source of pain and bewilderment. "Why won't they see that I am hurt?" she would plead in the privacy of our bedroom.

"Because you don't act that way," I'd reply.

"You just want me to be strong, so you can't allow yourself to see me the way I really am!" she would yell, and then begin to weep.

These fights would escalate, and I would worry that our shouting was frightening our children, who were at that time still small. When I'd try to get her to lower her voice, she would explode. "Stop *shushing* me! I'm not going to stop saying what I see and believe, just because you don't want me to say it! Women are supposed to be quiet and accepting, aren't they? But we aren't in your Sanford, Maine, repressed-culture household any more, are we?" It was difficult to disagree with her without its becoming yet one more example of how she had always been treated.

•   •   •

The marriage didn't work out, but the separation is great.
Gossip columnist Liz Smith reporting on a California couple

Not all of the challenges we dealt with in those days were personal in their origin. If you had had to name a time and place that made marriage difficult, it would have been California in the late sixties and early seventies. We were surrounded by claims that relationships should provide pleasure, or even joy, and that each party to them was to do his or her *own thing*. If it worked out, according to one motto of the time, great! If not, it "couldn't be helped." Open marriage—

the freedom to have other sexual relationships while maintaining the marriage—was being promoted as both sensible and liberating. We both agreed that one partner was a challenge enough for us, and we stayed monogamous—though not without feeling like a couple that was fox-trotting in a room full of rock-'n'-rollers.

Looking back on us, I wonder why we didn't recognize sooner the almost surreal quality of that time. One of our friends-spent an evening in 1970 talking to us enthusiastically—and invitingly, I thought—about the new sexual freedom that he and his wife had discovered by "opening" their marriage. He said that he was by himself, that very evening, because his wife just happened to be with her new lover. He talked about how much freer he felt. And then, inexplicably, he burst into tears. He apologized and admitted sheepishly that he still had hang-ups.

We were surprised to realize one day that we had both, independently of one another, fallen into a strange habit: Whenever we spoke of our lives, we said, not that we were "married" but that we were "*still* married." Talk about a society in transition! The world we lived in had gone almost overnight from one where singles were wallflowers and lonely hearts to one where they were swingers. These were years when everyone, it sometimes seemed, was divorcing. (Even Dear Abby, for heaven's sake!) In the airport we bumped into an acquaintance who had written a book in which he had talked about what a fulfilling marriage he had, and there he was, headed for Hawaii with a "friend."

In *Future Shock*, Alvin Toffler had written about "serial marriages" as the logical pattern for the future, arguing that as they became more common, "we [would] begin to characterize people not in terms of their present marital status, but in terms of their marriage career or trajectory." He went on to suggest some of the points at which the trajectory might change: beginning a trial marriage, ending it and deciding whether to continue or switch, deciding whether to have a family, deciding what to do after the children leave home, deciding what to do after retirement. "Of course," he added offhandedly, "there will be some who, through luck, interpersonal skill and

high intelligence, will find it possible to make long-lasting monogamous marriages work."[1] Feeling fresh out of skill and intelligence
about such matters, we hoped that we'd be lucky.

On our twentieth anniversary, we wanted to have a big party that
included more than our little circle of good friends, so we invited
people we had known during various periods in our life. One couple's invitation was returned: They had split, and neither was at the
address we had used; another woman said that her husband had just
moved out and she wasn't feeling much like socializing; yet another
couple couldn't join us because they were going to be away at a couple's retreat that weekend, trying to work things out.

Ironically, the years around 1980 were relatively happy ones for us.
Mondi's career as a therapist was firmly established and starting to
thrive, and I had just written *Transitions*. Our teen-age daughters
were doing pretty well in high school, and life in the rural community where we were living was interesting. We even gave a talk on
long-term marriages at a local church center. (Perhaps we had fallen
in love with our own title: *Couples in Transition, or How to Change
Places in a Badly Overloaded Canoe, with a Brush-up Swimming Lesson, Just in Case.*)

People started asking us, "How do you guys stay married?" At first
the question pleased me; I was happily surprised to find that, in spite
of what Mondi sometimes called my "lack of relatedness," we were
accomplishing something that many others couldn't. But I was also
confused. Was our success because we had chosen well, or because
(under the surface conflicts) we were deeply committed, or because
we were masochistic? Or was it that we had limited imaginations and
low levels of hormonal activity?

In our conversations about being still-married, Mondi and I began to speculate about the ingredients of marital longevity. Her therapy patients were constantly talking about their marriage difficulties,
and before we knew it we had written out our ideas into a prospectus
for a book on the subject. In spite of some modest success with
speaking and writing about transition, I was still searching for something about which I could be an expert. And we *had* been married

longer than most of our friends. When the publisher sent us a contract and a small advance, we took it to be a sign from heaven.

Something over a year later we had a manuscript—though not a book, since the publisher who agreed to publish it was bought out by a group that culled the lists of titles and, in the process, canceled our book. In retrospect, I'd have to say that it is just as well that the book was tossed out because it really wasn't as good as we liked to think it was. But at the time it was a huge setback to our plan to become experts on long-term relationships.

Even though in retrospect I don't regard the book as a good one, the *experience* of writing it was priceless. It drove home to me the fact that we had a serious power struggle within our marriage. The struggle surfaced when I secretly rewrote things that Mondi had written. I even had the gall to claim that I was doing it so that she wouldn't be embarrassed when the book was published. The truth was that I was utterly unable to collaborate on something that I cared about. It didn't help that I had too high an opinion of my own writing skill to turn the task over to her, and too much fear of her emotionality to talk honestly with her about the problem.

At that time (in the early eighties) we were gradually becoming more unstable as a couple, since we were even then in the middle of the second big power transition of our married years. The first had occurred when, encouraged by reading Carl Rogers, she had complained of our lack of communication and announced that she needed more from me and from our relationship. The second was still taking shape, but it had been triggered by our joining the community. Although the decision to do so had been mutual, Mondi was unhappy with some aspects of our new life from the start. She often ruminated about why she had "sold out" to me and occasionally would get so fed up that she would announce that she wanted to leave the community.

We would return from our all-day Monday meetings—we were very big on *process* in those days—and Mondi would be boiling over with frustration at the way in which issues got swept under the rug and the way that power was exercised but denied, not to mention the sexist statements and actions that were tolerated. And the way that people got away with not following the rules we set up for ourselves made her just furious! But what made her unhappiest was the way in which (as she saw it) I could do no wrong, while she was criticized by other community members for almost everything she did. "You're some kind of crown prince," she would complain bitterly. "I don't know how you do it, but you just *deflect* criticism. You put yourself *beyond* criticism."

Now, you couldn't live with five psychotherapists and as many more professionally trained amateurs without picking up a few ideas about how people worked, so I was psychologically hip enough to see (and heavy-handed enough to point out) that her experience of me in the community was very like her experience of her brother in her childhood family. Needless to say, I was pleased with myself at this insight. And needless to say, she was (once again) deeply hurt.

The difficulty was that, while she loved most of the community members individually, she was deeply ambivalent about living in the group that they formed. I, on the other hand, had never been in a group that felt so natural and comfortable. I had spent my life worrying that I didn't fit in anywhere, but in the community I had finally found a *home*.

As my early thinking about transition and lifetime took shape, the group encouraged me to develop and to communicate my ideas. In the first year the community even subsidized me to the tune of $1,000 a month while I started my new "Being In Transition" seminars. Mondi, who was scared that I was going to turn this career detour into a permanent income-free zone, sought in vain to find allies among these same people. They sympathized with her feeling— Lord, everyone sympathized with *everyone's* feelings in our community!—but they refused to get upset with or put pressure on me.

Mondi had a point. The community was, for most of us, a permissive parent that treated us like big, wonderful kids. We all had to face reality in the end, but during the difficult time of transition, when we were letting go of an old life and finding a new one, we enjoyed just the kind of support that people in transition long for. It was, however, exactly the kind of support that Mondi had never had, and she believed that in my case it encouraged the unrealistic and self-centered part of my personality. Under the surface of our disagreement was a subtle but large shift in power, whereby I regained some of the self-confidence and conviction that I had lost when our communication project had relocated power into her hands.

In the midst of this second of our transitions as a couple, it was hard for her not to see the community as her rival for my favor. She worried that if her rival won, I would drift further and further into this self-exploratory void and not support my family. If her rival won, she lost; and so she began to want to leave. That frightened me, since I was just starting to find the new direction I had come there looking for. In desperation, I said that I couldn't stop her from leaving, but that this was the life I had been searching for and that I was staying. I kept trying to figure out how to take my stand in a less threatening way, but like some unmanned homing device, the discussion kept coming back around to that: I was choosing the community over her.

As I write these things, I wonder if I am exaggerating our conflict. But then I go back and read one of the journals I kept at that time. "I'm really discouraged," begins one entry—those words show up in many of them, actually. The journal entry continues to catalog my experience:

- I am overwhelmed by her intensity.
- I pull punches and deny my real feelings when I talk to her.
- Then she says I am talking double-talk, that she can't trust what I say because it changes and conflicts with how I behave.
- I say that I *am not feeling hostile!* I say it in what I have to admit is a hostile tone of voice.
- I talk to whatever therapist I am seeing then, and she says that I do sound just a bit hostile—but that maybe I have some reason for being that way.
- I share the second part with her later, but leave out the part

about the therapist's sensing my hostility. I report it as a validation of my feelings.

- But the validation just proves to her that I am pulling the
wool over the therapist's eyes. "You choose therapists who
won't challenge you, Bill."

And around and around we went, spurred on by the pain of a
transition neither of us understood and that both of us were scared
to talk about.

Although these exchanges were all too real, they were not the only
talks we had. There were also warm and caring times, as well as times
of great fun and humor. One side of her was sensitive and very wise,
and it was that side that came out in her work with her patients. She
was an extraordinary psychotherapist, able to draw on her own
knowledge of pain to talk to her patients at a very deep level. The letters I received from some of them after she died were profoundly
moving, and I knew exactly what they were talking about, because I
too had known that side of her.

I often felt that her patients got the best of her, but I had to admit that she had been the first—and for a long time the only—person who could draw me out and bring fun into my life. We even
had fun writing the book on long-term relationships, laughing as
we recalled the experiences we had been through as a couple. My
gradual disenchantment with life in the community—those meetings really *were* too much, especially when they dealt with one family's dogs pooping on another family's lawn—led me ultimately to
see things much more her way. Finally we decided to leave the
community and move closer to San Francisco, partly to make my
increasingly frequent travel easier.

Our financial arrangements within the community were very
complicated, and getting out was a bit like extricating yourself from
a pile of barbed wire. It took us several years to do so, in fact, but in
1985 we finally left the community and moved to Mill Valley. That
change put us back into transition, but this time we both gained so
much from the change that the transition was less difficult. It also

coincided with the increasing success of my business and her desire to enter the certification program at the San Francisco Jung Institute. The move both reinforced and reflected the third big transition in our married life—our return to an ordinary lifestyle and a renewed professional commitment after eleven years of country living in the community.

•   •   •

One advantage of marriage, it seems to me, is that when you fall out of love with [your partner]. . . it keeps you together until you maybe fall in again.

Judith Viorst

Shortly after we finished our manuscript, Mondi had started a new round of analysis with a psychiatrist. She had seen many psychotherapists of one kind or another, but from the beginning she felt that her work with George was going to be different. He was a very empathetic man of about my age, a man who had gone through a lot of difficult experiences in his own life and who seemed to understand her. He was also the first male therapist she had worked with, and that was important. She had always been frightened to let herself become emotionally dependent on a man.

Very early in their work she told him that she knew that her fear of men came partly from her worry that if she allowed herself to be close to them or to show her attraction to them in any way, the result would be that things would become sexual. But she was tired of being burdened by that fear, and she wanted to get over it. She was looking for someone both sensitive enough to understand her and strong enough to stand up to her. George seemed to fit the bill, both ways. "He really gets it," she reported.

Her therapy with him became enormously important to her, for she found that he offered the kind of total emotional support that she had never before had from anyone. He really, really understood her, she said. Even from the outside, it was clear that he was providing her with something she had never had before. Her work with him was the most important thing in her life.

The therapy went on for several years, during which she was accepted as a candidate at the C. G. Jung Institute of San Francisco, where George was a senior analyst. The institute required that candidates work with both a male and a female analyst in the course of their training, and Mondi came home one day to say that she and George had mutually decided that it would be good for her to work with a woman who had been supervised by George during her training. So she stopped seeing George for analysis.

Not very long after that, Mondi and I went out to dinner with two psychologist friends of ours. In the course of the dinner, the man of the couple began taking a kind of devil's advocate position on the question of sexual relations between an analyst and a patient. Was it *always* wrong? he asked. Weren't there situations in which it might be all right, or even helpful? What if the sexual relations didn't actually begin until the therapeutic work concluded? Was it still wrong? I remember wondering if he was having an affair with a client. It also wasn't clear to me how much he believed what he was saying and how much he was just trying to be provocative, but Mondi was obviously upset by the position he was taking. I can't remember what she said, but as someone who had experienced some sexual abuse as a child, this kind of talk was very painful for her to hear.

After we left the restaurant, we had driven only three or four blocks when she blurted out, "I have to tell you that George and I slept together. It's over now. But for a while, we were having sex."

I felt as though the car had just run into a wall. I was stunned. Then a cold chill ran through my body. "Sex. You had sex?"

"Yes."

"How many times?" It felt like a stupid question, but somehow I had to ask it.

"Quite a few. Once a week. For several months."

I can't remember the rest of the drive home, and the next several weeks are faint in my memory. We talked about what had happened a number of times. I had to talk about it, but the talk never made me feel better. Sometimes our conversation would collapse under the weight of my feelings of hurt and betrayal. I felt crushed, and there were times when I mistrusted every word she uttered. I hurt in ways that I couldn't previously have imagined, a kind of bone-ache that made me want to crawl into bed and cover my head. Sometimes I would sink into self-doubt and start to blame myself for what had happened.

She made it clear that she wished that she had not done it, that she felt violated by this man who promised to help her through her fears of men. He had presented their sexual relationship as an important part of her healing from her early experiences. It was something special and very intimate between them: "No one needs to know about this. They wouldn't understand," he had said.

I had moments of being able to sympathize with the terrible hurt and shame that she felt at this violation of her trust. And I had times of being able to understand just how vulnerable she had been to such a "loving" authority figure. But there were also many times when I just hated her for what she had done.

But I was also frightened for her. She sank into a depression that was so profound that I wondered if she was going to kill herself. When I asked her, she reassured me—but in a way that was not very reassuring. Yes, she felt very depressed. And, yes, she had thought that it would almost be easier "just to disappear," as she put it. But, no, she had not even considered doing anything specific. She wasn't going to kill herself, she said. It didn't sound as though she said it with much conviction, though.

•   •   •

Pain–has an Element of Blank–
It cannot recollect
When it begun–or if there were
A time when it was not–

Emily Dickinson

Although my fear kept me from pressing the issue for a long time, I grew increasingly upset by not seeing any signs that she could understand and acknowledge what this experience had done to me. She seemed entirely oblivious to how my trust had been violated. When I tried to talk to her about the impact on me of what she had done, how deeply disillusioned with her I felt, she simply said that she couldn't deal with that now. I was in therapy myself, she pointed out, and I ought to talk to my therapist about those feelings.

The demand that *we* needed to talk was one she couldn't grant. It was not until almost ten years later that we found a way to talk about it. Even then I found that my need to be seen as a person who had also been wounded in the incident was taken by her as a sign that, when the chips were down, I just thought of myself and didn't provide her with the support she needed in her terrible crisis.

"I guess you couldn't do that," she said.

"I guess I couldn't," I replied. "Not then."

•   •   •

Life never presents us with anything which may not be looked upon as a fresh starting point, no less than as a termination.

André Gide

On one level, our lives began to move forward again. She reported George to the Jung Institute of which they were both members and to the state agency that licensed therapists. After much soul-searching, she decided to sue him to recover the money she had paid him for the "therapy" that turned out to be little more than having sex with her. As she began to do those things, as well as to stand up in a members' meeting at the institute to tell everyone what had happened and what she was doing about it, she began to get some of her strength back. She spoke publicly and courageously, and while some of the older men came to George's defense, most of the members of the institute were appalled at such a flagrant violation of therapeutic ethics.

When it later turned out that Mondi was the *fifth* patient with whom he had had sexual relations, the balance of opinion swung clearly in her favor. She, in some sense, felt vindicated, although whenever she intuited that anyone doubted her absolute innocence, she could get very upset. But she generally felt that she had resolved a bad, bad situation as well as she could. She could even wonder if she might not have saved still further patients from having her experience. She began to make notes for an autobiographically based book she planned to write about how destructive sexual violations of trust are. She had just started putting together an outline for the book when she was diagnosed with cancer.

•   •   •

Its beauty does not hide its flaws, its flaws do not hide its beauties.

Confucius, on the subject of jade

I have tried to think of how I could tell the story of my transitions without sharing this aspect of my life story, for it is still very painful for me to recall it. But coming less than five years before she died, and having had an enormous impact on our relationship, the memory of it kept looming up in front of me again and again as I wrote, whichever direction I turned. As the source of the fourth of our big marital transitions, I simply could not bypass it. It represented an ending for both of us: I lost the kind of instinctive trust in her that I had had before, and she lost a view of herself as someone who knew herself too well to "get mixed up in something like that."

The events surrounding making her illicit relationship with her therapist public were the triggers for even further transitions. Even the people who supported her at the institute felt that she ought to put her candidacy on hold while she (and the institute) sorted out what had happened. So she lost the chance to become an analyst on the same schedule with her peers and within the time she had hoped. She also became, to some of the analysts, a symbol of The New Candidate, who was more problematic than the Old Boys had been, and she found herself playing an unintended role in the debates about how that institution ought to certify its analyst members and guard against future abuses of therapeutic power. George was expelled from the institute and stripped of his license by the state, but that did not end the debates.

As more people heard what had happened, I became visible to a wider circle as the man whose wife had slept with her analyst. For months, I felt acutely uncomfortable around anyone who knew our secret, and I blamed her for exposing me to such shame. But gradually, my anger and the shame on which it was based disappeared. We began to talk more comfortably again and time did its work of healing. (Time is, in the end, the only healer. Everything that can consciously be done to help can only clear the ground for time to do its work.)

I discovered in the process that forgiveness, in its most significant form, does not involve ceasing to be angry at someone who has hurt you. It involves ceasing to be angry with *life* for the hurt. For the condition that forgiveness addresses is not so much interpersonal estrangement as it is the alienation of individuals from their own lives and from the developmental lessons that those lives provide. The interpersonal aspect of forgiveness is the outcome of recovering a vital relation to your own life. When one has accepted one of life's painful gifts, blaming the person who delivered it is not so much a moral flaw as it is a bit of self-indulgence.

Even with forgiveness, however, this was a huge transition for our marriage. Like any such transition, it left us a different couple than when it found us. We felt more fragile—closer in some ways, but also with unanswered questions and unspoken misgivings that we never managed to resolve. We hardly even tried to, since our final transition—caused by her cancer—came along so soon.

When we were talking more easily again, I realized that although she was through the practical crisis, she was now dealing with a deeper one that showed no sign of abating. Her experience of being violated had laid bare her essential self-rejection and despair. These were aspects of her makeup that she had sometimes talked about, usually when she was asking why people didn't understand how vulnerable and hurt she was. But she had never before let me see directly those dark places that she had hidden so long and so well.

I would go down to our bedroom when I thought she was napping and find her lying on our bed, weeping. I would talk with her, but she was almost mute at such times and could do little more than hold my hand. At other times she would pick at her fingers almost absentmindedly until they bled. She would draw pictures of herself as a tiny, naked infant exposed under a winter sky. She wrote and wrote and wrote in her notebook, and although we agreed that those writings were off limits to me—and later, that I would burn them (as I did) after she died—she read me one or two passages that were so deeply depressed that I could hardly imagine what it was like to feel that way about yourself.

●   ●   ●

For one human being to love another: That is perhaps the most difficult of all our tasks, the ultimate, the last test and proof, the work for which all other work is but preparation.

Rainer Maria Rilke

This was the woman that I came to know so deeply in those months before she died. Before that, I could not understand how close to the edge of the abyss she had always lived. After that, I ran back through the conflicts and misunderstandings we had had and understood many of them far better. I got beyond the disillusionment that I had felt when she first told me about what she and George had done and found a deeper experience—disenchantment.

I woke up from the enchantment, the spell I had been under. I really saw this woman I had been living with for all these years for the first time, saw her in all of her pain and self-rejection and longing. In so doing, I came to love her in a way I had never loved her before. Love, after all, has far more to do with seeing someone clearly and accepting them fully for who they actually are than it does with feeling attracted to or liking them.

This is the woman who died in the bed next to me, the woman who made jokes about tripping out on her morphine until a couple of hours before she died. This is the woman whose death left such a huge hole in my life, whose death threw me back to a time in my life before I had met her and found out that I could fall in love and care for someone. This is the woman that I said good-bye to again and again and again in the months before she died, the woman whose ashes my daughters and I scattered under the oak trees on the western slopes of Mt. Tamalpais.

It was the memory of this complicated and sorrowful woman that was reawakened by the black feathers on my walk that morning; had they been white or gray or blue feathers, I would have known they were not from her. This is the woman who, when she was dying, read those books about the different spirit topographies through which the soul is supposed to pass before it can finally rest in peace. As I have already said, Mondi was fascinated by those accounts, and a little frightened by them too. "But I've gone to some very dark places," she said with a faint smile just a week before she died, "so I'm sure I'll be O.K." I told her that I, too, thought she would.

seven

The Archetype of the Journey

*Archetypes resemble the beds of rivers: dried up
because the water has deserted them, though it may
return at any time. An archetype is something like an
old watercourse along which the water of life flowed
for a time, digging a deep channel for itself. The longer
it flowed the deeper the channel, and the more likely it
is that sooner or later the water will return.*

C. G. Jung

I have referred to my marriage as a "journey," although I know that to some people that metaphor will sound like California-speak. I don't use the term casually, however. I would argue that the journey is a profound symbol, an archetype that has etched itself on the human consciousness for two reasons.[1] First, because human beings have taken so many literal journeys during our time on the earth that the image has worked its way deep into our psyches; and, second, because in its image of moving from one place to another while also going deeper within oneself, the journey captures a powerful truth about transition that (especially today) we need to be able to express. Journeys form the thematic core of many of our most compelling literary works. Think of Homer's *Odyssey*, Dante's *Divine Comedy*, and the Old Testament book of Exodus. Think of Steinbeck's *The Grapes of Wrath*, Virgil's *The Aeneid*, and Whitman's *Song of the Open Road*. Think of Kerouac's *On the Road*, Verne's *Around the World in Eighty Days* and Forster's *A Passage to India*. Think of Jason and the Story of the Golden Fleece, Theseus going into the Labyrinth to slay the Minotaur, and the fabled search for El Dorado. Think of *Star Trek* and *The Canterbury Tales* and *Alice in Wonderland*.

The journey motif also gives an added imaginative power to many historical events, as well. Think how these events have captured our imaginations: the voyage of Columbus to the New World, the Pilgrims' search for a new home, the astronauts' flight to the moon, and Lindbergh's flight across the Atlantic, the Mormons' trek to Utah, and the 49ers' journey to the gold fields of California. There were Marco Polo, Lewis and Clark, and Stanley's search for Dr. Livingston. There were the great Silk Route, the Oregon Trail, and The Trail of Tears. Everywhere it appears, the journey taps into something stirring and deep within us.

The stories of journeying often begin with a state of affairs in which life—some individual's life, at least—has run down, gone dead, or fallen apart. In other words, they start as the transitions that they mimic do—with an ending. Melville described that state at the opening of *Moby-Dick*, one of the greatest journey-novels, in these words:

Whenever I feel myself growing grim about the mouth; whenever it is a damp, drizzly November in my soul; whenever I find myself involuntarily pausing before coffin warehouses, and bringing up the rear of every funeral I meet. . . then I account it high time to get to sea as soon as I can. This is my substitute for pistol and ball. With a philosophical flourish Cato throws himself upon his sword; I quietly take to the ship.

Journeys finish when the white whale is finally encountered or when the Joads get to California or when Odysseus gets back to

Ithaca: That is, they finish when the goal has been reached. And yet, it always turns out, the goal was only an external representation for some inner place, some state that the journeying person needs to attain. In the language of *going somewhere,* journeys tell us about the unnamable *nowhere* that is not a place but a way of being.

Since it is so pervasive, it is not surprising that transition shapes the journey-stories I have cited. Transition is, in fact, the dynamic element that makes these stories more than narratives about trips and turns them, in fact, into myths. One of our modern misunderstandings of myth is the notion that the mythic imagination is no longer at work in the world. The Greeks had myths, and so did the Jews of the Old Testament. Romans, yes; Celtic peoples, yes; Asians of the early historical ages, yes; native Americans, yes; and ditto the indigenous peoples of Africa and Australia. Though we don't usually associate myths with modern American thought, we do indeed have our own. Consider the powerfully mythic story written at the opening of the twentieth century by L. Frank Baum. It was made into one of Hollywood's most memorable movies in the late 1930's. You know the story. And because you already know it, I want to tell this modern American myth about transition in a way that is a little unusual.

Myths are often said to contain some of the characteristics of dreams, because they both draw their power from layers of the psyche where the archetypes make their home. Some students of the dreamworld argue that everything in a dream actually represents some aspect of the dreamer. A woman who is dreaming about a man, for example, is also dreaming about the male part of herself, which Carl Jung called her "animus." The man who dreams about a little dog is also dreaming about the part of himself that is like a little dog—playful, instinctive, not always obedient, but also wanting to please: the doggy part.

So I am going to tell the myth in question as though it were a dream that you, yourself, had. I will interject interpretive comments of my own, but I will put those in italics so as not to confuse you. Here goes.

•   •   •

The trip becomes "a journey" after you have lost your luggage.

Anonymous

You are a little girl and you live in a flat, dry land. The rains have stopped, and the ground is cracking open under the hot sun. All the green life that used to cover the earth is dying, and everything is dusty and gray. *The image of the dry, wasted land is a very old one in literature. The story of Oedipus begins with it, and it shows up again in the biblical Valley of the Bones. T. S. Eliot wrote a famous poem about it called "The Waste Land." It represents a metaphorical vision of a world that has gone dead, a life that has come to the end of its tether. Whether or not one is ready to admit it, it is time to let go—to leave behind whatever one is holding on to.*

You are playing with your little dog, Toto, when you notice a dark funnel cloud moving across the fields toward you. Your aunt and uncle, with whom you live, have told you over and over: "If a cyclone ever comes, get down into the cyclone cellar under the house as fast as you can!" So you grab Toto and start to run for the house. *Naturally, when trouble comes, you try to save yourself and whatever you care most about. Even though things may be going very badly in your life, the parental voices in your head (and the part of you that listens to them) would rather keep things going as they are than to let your life head off in some completely unknown direction. After all, the counsel that you were following was given—how often were you told?—for 'your own good.'*

You *almost* make it into the cellar. *And if you had, the storm would have blown over and there would have been no story. (Of course, you'd also still be in the Waste Land, wondering what to do with your life, wouldn't you?) When the misfortune occurs, you often imagine that you missed the "good" path that you ought to have taken and that you were stuck with the "unfortunate" alternative. Later, however, you sometimes come to see that your "misfortune" was actually your salvation.*

Just as you are about to duck into the safe hiding place, Toto hops out of your arms and runs into the house—which is, you realize to your dismay, now shaking and rattling and about to be yanked off its foundations by the wind. You have a split second to make a choice— no weighing risks or brainstorming creative alternatives—and you choose to try to rescue Toto. No sooner do you dash after him into the house, though, than an enormous gust of wind twirls it up into the air. It spirals up and up, with you and Toto in it, through the clouds, completely out of the universe of Kansas. *You often intend to stay with the life you are living, but then something catastrophic breaks in and sends you reeling. You lose your life as you had known it and find yourself facing a future that you cannot imagine. Now, you'd think that, with the drought and the bad crops and all, you had enough bad luck: But then there comes the cyclone! Talk about bad timing. Yet it turns out that this was a timely misfortune. And even within this event, there is a littler timely accident—Toto's escape. But we are getting ahead of our story.*

The house spins wildly through the sky, farther and farther from the world you knew. After a long time, though, it begins to descend and finally comes thumping to a stop in the strangest place you've ever seen: strange, beautiful flowers; strange, little people; and a strange, beautiful "witch" named Glenda. You look out the window and (in one of the great *neutral zone* statements of all time) you say to your doggy, little fellow-traveler, "I don't think we're in Kansas any more, Toto." *After the ending, the loss, the letting go, you always find yourself in a strange place. The neutral zone is never a place on a map. It's inside the mirror or down the rabbit hole or just through the back of the wardrobe. It's light-years away, and it is no farther away than your thumb. It's not a geographical place, but rather a whole new dimension to experience.*

Your house has landed on, and killed, a "bad witch," and the people of Oz are delighted. You ask how to get back to Kansas—which is all you care about. (Fix things. Get them back the way they were!) Glenda says that she doesn't know how to do that—but that the great Wizard of Oz probably will, because he knows everything. She gives you the dead witch's ruby slippers for good luck and sends you off on a your quest to find out how to get back to Kansas. You can't miss the route to the Wizard's Emerald City, she says. It's a bright yellow brick road. *Well, at least someone knows how to get back, and at least now you know how to find the expert who does. It's all a question of how-to (the method-way) and you'll find the expert who knows how-to too.*

So, off you go. In short order, you encounter three strange traveling companions: a scarecrow, with straw instead of brains; a tin woodsman, whose metal body is complete except for a heart; and a cowardly lion, who looks fierce but is really a scaredy-cat. *In other words, you take along on all your journeys the part of you that isn't smart enough to handle the task that life gives you; the part that doesn't know what you feel about whatever happens to you; and the part that is faking it because it is so insecure and self-doubting. (Some of us have more of one part or more of another: In our culture, men have traditionally been seen as deficient in feeling, and women have been treated as scatterbrained. And everyone is trying to succeed by putting up the good front.) Whatever your deficiencies, however, an expert will know how to put you right. The Wizard has the technique.*

The journey to Oz (*which, incidentally, was the "O-Z" on the bottom file-cabinet drawer that caught Baum's eye when he was originally making up this story for his children in his office*) was difficult, as quests always are. There were ditches and rivers to cross. There were the Kalidahs, a forest of trees with arm-branches that grabbed you as you passed. There was even a field of poppies (*opium poppies!*) that almost aborted the journey right there by putting the lion to sleep. (*On many quests, it takes so long to reach your destination that you drift off your path and forget why you ever undertook the journey in the first place.*) But finally, you all arrive at the Emerald City of Oz where the Wizard lives. At last you'll find out how to get back to Kansas! *Quests are difficult. But, then, wisdom is valuable and it's worth fighting for. Otherwise, everyone would have it and it wouldn't be so valuable, would it?*

The visit to the Wizard doesn't go so well, however. The shimmering green color everywhere makes it hard to see things clearly. The Wizard speaks out of clouds of smoke, and his words are puzzling.

He leaves no doubt, however, that your quest isn't done yet. It seems that you must go into a dark land where "there is no road." Worse yet, the challenges of the previous journey were minor-league ones compared with what you encounter in this second journey: flying monkeys that swoop down and carry away Toto, and a witch that scatters the stuffing of your scarecrow, that dents and scrunches up the metal of the tin woodsman, and that calls the lion's bluff and locks him up in a cage. And you, little girl, are turned into her housemaid. That's it; the game's over! *These quest stories often have a first stage where the quester fails, as if to say that at that point the journey hasn't done its work on you yet. You aren't ready for the big-time because your transformation isn't complete. But rather than getting this news in a message from some Office of the Dean of Life, who says you have to repeat the "course" you've been taking, you get it as a deeply discouraging setback, a disaster. (Yet another loss!) You have to "hit bottom," as they stay in the Twelve-Step programs, before you are ready to learn.*

But it is always darkest just before the. . . yah-da-yah-da. One day when you are wet-mopping the witch's kitchen, she pushes you just a little too far. Thinking back, you don't even know what makes you do it, but you pick up the pail of water and dump it on her head. And she melts away into nothing. *How did you know to do that? You really can't say. It just came to you. The breakthrough wasn't planned out. It just "emerged." You could have read all the self-help books in the store, and you wouldn't have found the instructions for this particular case. It just happened. But rather than puzzling over that strange turn of events, you can't wait to get back to your journey. That old Wizard thought you couldn't succeed. Well, you showed him. You are One Great Quester!*

You dash out and retrieve your companions, restuffing the Scarecrow and smoothing out the crinkles in the Tin Woodsman. You reassure the Cowardly Lion that he really is a Big Brave Boy. You rescue Toto and make him promise to stay out of trouble from now on (what is it with that naughty dog, anyway?), and you all march back to the Emerald City like knights returning from a successful crusade.

The Wizard will certainly have to tell you the secret of getting back to Kansas now! *You still view this whole experience as Getting-the-Answer-from-the-Wizard, and see the nasty episode with the Wicked Witch as just a temporary detour. So you stomp back into the Emerald Palace expecting to be told what a Smart Young Girl you are. But when you arrive. . .*

. . . the Wizard turns out to be less than thrilled to see you. He equivocates. He puffs out cloud after cloud of that damn green smoke. He hems and haws and. . . just then Toto tips over a screen and reveals the scraggly little man behind it making his voice big and boomy by talking into a megaphone. *Wizard indeed! Just an ordinary three-for-a-dime loser who looks a lot like that sleight-of-hand snake-oil vendor that you saw in the carnival, back in Kansas, just before the cyclone struck. He says that he is, basically—if you want to put it into a single word—a fake. The green? It was in the glasses that he made you wear. The disembodied sound: He's a ventriloquist. The visual effects: literally, smoke and mirrors. The witches, interestingly enough, are apparently real. They have power. But the wizard. . . he just does tricks.*

Disenchanting as this discovery is, you hardly stop to think about it right then, because in the next breath he says that in just about five minutes he is going to take off in a hot-air balloon ("*hot air,*" get it?) for Kansas. What luck! There is just time for a hasty Awards Ceremony, where the un-Wizard gives the Scarecrow a diploma (which turns out to be all that he lacked to be a Person with Brains); and gives the Tin Woodsman an old tick-tock alarm clock to put inside his big tin can of a chest (the sound would show that there *was* a heart in there, after all); and the Lion (who only really needed a public affirmation of his courage to become officially "brave") was given a medal. *There. A solution for every problem. The broken are made whole again, just as they are supposed to be at the end of a quest. All those wounded parts of you got what they came for. And you, you finally get a ride back to Kansas!*

You go out to the launchpad. The balloon is tugging at its rope moorings. You say good-bye to your fellow pilgrims. A journey like this creates bonds, and you will miss them. The Wizard climbs into the balloon gondola, like some forerunner of Richard Branson. You and Toto hop in; you'll be in Kansas before you can say,. . . "Hey, where is Toto going? Stop him! And, wait. Don't let the balloon go off without me! Toto. Wizard. Toto. Wizard. Oh, no. Disaster. Again." Your last chance to get home is gone. And once again, it's Toto! What is that damned little dog trying to do to you, anyway? *There is a figure in dreams that some analysts call "the helpful animal," a little creature that, at critical moments, does something that turns the whole dream in a new direction. Such a figure is a representation of the less-than (or, better, other-than) rational part of the dreamer that somehow knows what needs to happen for the dream-tale to end as it should—and for the journey to be successful in ways that the pilgrim may not at the time be able to understand and certainly is powerless to make happen. Toto is a "helpful animal," in that sense, for he insures that Dorothy both goes to Oz when she needs to take that journey and that she gets home in the right way when it is the right time to return. And the timing is the whole story, for just as the journey into the neutral zone occurred when the Waste Land situation showed that the life forces had evaporated and that it was time for an ending, so the journey could not finish until it had done its work. To keep it from ending prematurely, Toto ran away again. O.K., but, hey, how are you going to get back?*

You look up pitifully at your vanishing hope, and you hear a voice behind you. It is Glenda, the Good Witch. "You don't need the balloon," she says in effect. "You've got those ruby slippers—the ones you got from the Wicked Witch that you squashed when you landed. Just knock your heels together three times, and wish yourself back in Kansas. You try it. Snick. Snick. Snick. And whoosh. . . *After all this questing, you find out that the power was within you. You thought that the Wizard had it. You had it. You thought that you had to perform external labors. The answer was on your own feet. But wait! Does that mean that the whole journey was unnecessary? That you could have stepped out of the storm-carried house and snick-snick-snick, gone home right then? Well, yes and no. Yes, technically. But the story wouldn't have let you do that. (Stories have a life and a wisdom of their own.) Back then, you weren't ready yet. The experience that we are calling the "transitional experience" hadn't yet done its work on you. If you had gone home back when you first landed, you would have found things just as dead as you left them. But having completed your journey, you return to Kansas and find that. . . .*

. . . the fields are green again. The old gray house has been repaired and repainted bright white. Your aunt and uncle aren't gray, wasted people any more. Rain has fallen on the Waste Land, and it has been renewed. A new life-force has pushed through every living thing. A new beginning has occurred.

• • •

The passage of the mythological hero may be [from one geographical place to another, but] fundamentally it is inward—into the depths where obscure resistances are overcome, and long lost, forgotten powers are revivified, to be made available for the transfiguration of the world.

Joseph Campbell

Both as a book and as a movie, *The Wizard of Oz* is a memorable myth of the transitional journey, which renews life by cycling it through an ending, then into a period in "another land" which is the neutral zone, and then back—with new life and energy—into beginning a new chapter of existence. To say that *The Wizard of Oz* follows the same path taken by an individual in transition is simply to say that growth and development always begin with the destruction of the old state of affairs or the old stage of development. Dorothy's world is plunged into transition when it has exhausted its natural resources for development. She regains such resources only by turning aside from the path that she has been following. She plunges, unintentionally and against her will, into the fertile wilderness of the neutral zone where she discovers (as usual, apparently by accident) what she needs to know to take the next step in her development.

The wisdom of the everyday world always calls on the traveler to keep to the straight path and persevere toward the intended destination. But the Way Of Transition heads off in another direction. Another of these mythic journeyers was Dante, who had been exiled from both his home and his friends for being on the wrong side of a political fight in Florence at the end of the thirteenth century. In the opening lines of *The Divine Comedy,* he pictures himself as one who has lost the straight path and is lost in the middle of a dark wood. His guide, Virgil, takes him into the underworld (*you must go down before you can come up again. . . and end before you can begin anew*) through a gate over which was written the motto, *Give Up Hope, All Ye Who Enter Here.*

The point is not that there is no hope on the journey-path, for in fact Dante's version of it ends up in Paradiso. It is simply that what passes for "hope" when you are starting into transition is likely to be simply the fantasy that you can somehow return to your old life in Florence, or wherever your Kansas happens to be. What passes for hope is the fantasy that there's a way to get through this difficult squeeze-point between one life phase and the next with all your luggage. What passes for hope is that you'll be able to call the shots yourself and that you won't need a Toto. It is that the Wizard will give you a map marked "X—You Are Here," and that the hot-air balloons are running on a daily schedule now.

·   ·   ·

Boundary surfaces are everywhere the places where living formative processes can find a hold; be it in cell membranes, surfaces of contact between cells, where life forces are mysteriously present; in the great boundary surfaces between the current systems of the oceans, where various currents flow past each other in different directions—these are known to be particularly rich in fish; or at the infinitely extensive surfaces of the natural and artificial filter systems of the earth, where the water seeping through is purified and given back its vital qualities.

Theodore Schwenck

Transformation is the true destination of transition, whether it occurs in a myth or in an individual's everyday life. How transition does that is a mystery, but it somehow involves being in a boundary state, where you spend time near a boundary between one state and another, or one life-phase and the next. The borders of Oz are everywhere, although the price of passage to the other side is often nothing less than your life—at least your life as you have known it. And the yellow brick road, that they point out to you, is little more than an excuse to get you walking and an encouragement for those times when it's getting dark and cold and no emerald towers are in sight. And the Wizard is what is called a "helpful fiction," for no one else can really tell you the path that you must follow.

Although we are all following a way (in the *path* sense), there are no *ways* (in the *method* sense) to guide us on our journeying. You and I are headed to the same place, because both of us are on the way to transformation and life renewal. And yet each of us is on a unique and unreplicable path. And the Emerald City—or nirvana or self-actualization or whatever they're calling it this year—was only the come-on that convinced us to set forth. The outcome that justifies the journey is back at home in Kansas.

●   ●   ●

Prigogene coined the term 'dissipative structures' to focus attention on the inherent contradiction of the two descriptors. . . . Dissipation describes a loss, a process by which energy gradually ebbs away. Yet Prigogine discovered that such dissipative activity could play a constructive role in the creation of new structures. Dissipation didn't lead to the demise of a system. It was part of the process by which the system let go of its present form so that it could reemerge in a form better suited to the demands of the present environment.

Margaret Wheatley

The pattern of the journey is embedded in both the structure of nature and the processes of history. As Prigogine says in the epigraph quoted above, some categories of matter reveal its workings. Another scientist has explained that any system has a "critical parameter," and that parameter is what governs whether or not the system makes what, in the human world, could be called *a journey*. This parameter is, he writes, the "threshold [that] marks the point at which the least fluctuation can cause the system to leave its uniform stationary state. When this occurs, a fluctuation is amplified and drives the system to some new state."[2] Natural evolution itself operates in an analogous way.

So too, according to the great historian Arnold J. Toynbee, do the rise of great civilizations, for such flowerings occur as responses to some profound challenge from their natural or social environment. He calls that the process of Challenge and Response, and illustrates it with the case of Egypt's Nile Valley, where a sophisticated civilization arose after an earlier hunter-gatherer society had been devastated by climatic changes that turned temperate grasslands full of game and edible plants into arid desert. When that happened, Toynbee wrote "these heroic pioneers. . . plunged into the jungle-swamps of the valley bottoms, never before penetrated by man."

> To their neighbors, who took the alternative course [of leaving the Nile Valley entirely and becoming nomads], their venture must have seemed a forlorn hope; for in the outlived age when the area which was now beginning to turn into the Afrasian Steppe had been an earthly paradise, the Nilotic. . . jungle-swamp had been a forbidding and apparently impenetrable wilderness. As it turned out . . . the wantonness of nature was subdued by the works of man; the formless jungle-swamp made way for a pattern of ditches and embankments and fields; the lands of Egypt. . . were reclaimed from the wilderness, and the Egyptiac. . . society started on its great adventure.[3]

This societal example highlights several other aspects of the challenge-and-response pattern which journey stories dramatize. One is that the new developmental phase often requires the society or the individual to embrace a choice that did not even appear to *exist* under the old conditions. Another aspect to the challenge and response pattern that leads to a journey is that the individuals who take the easier course of action—often because it requires a more modest leap of imagination and a less sweeping rejection of the old outlook—view the more difficult, creative response as utterly foolhardy.

In such cases, the creative response on which the future was built was one that could really never have been considered until the situation changed beyond recognition. It was not just the external change, but rather an inner shift of outlook and a redefinition of possibility that combined with the outer changes to create a new "reality." So it is the confusing and distressing world left behind after an ending— whether by climate change in ancient Egypt or banishment in the case of Dante or Mondi's death in my own case—that provides conditions that make breakthroughs possible. At least, I *hoped* that my life fit that pattern and that my journey would bring me renewal.

But I had to admit that understanding how journeys actually do that was discomforting, because no matter how much I understood their dynamic, at some level I wanted to believe that there is a *there* there to reach and settle down at and enjoy. That notion is what keeps alive the fantasy about there being a (technique-type) way to bring about the results you want to achieve and a way to replicate that way once it has been discovered by someone else.

Here is an organizational example of that longing for a technique: A few years ago, at the European headquarters of a large high-tech corporation, the employees had become unproductive and were very dispirited. They complained about how their building was laid out, how it functioned, and how it felt to work in it. So the head of European Operations called them together and said that he was too busy to take on the responsibility for remodeling their work space himself, but that he was willing for them to do it if they wished.

At first they were hesitant: They didn't know enough about architecture or interior design; they didn't have the authority to spend the kind of money it would take; and they didn't know how to work with designers. With their poor morale and low energy, it was just all too much. But slowly they came to accept the idea that taking on the project themselves was the only way to get what they wanted, and they ultimately did it.

The process of figuring out how to do everything themselves was, of course, their greatest learning. For that reason, the result of their efforts was not only a building that was both efficient and beautiful, but also achieving a whole new self-confidence and sense of power. As their morale rose, their productivity did too. And in the process, they learned that morale and self-confidence is not produced by re-designed spaces but by the experience of taking a journey out of an old world, through the world of a strange and novel experience, and back again to the old (but now-renewed) world.

The news of their project and its results traveled throughout the international operations of the great company, and at the next company-wide meeting of general managers (which was, not coinci-dentally, held there at the European headquarters) the employees made a presentation to tell what they had done. In introducing the employees, their boss emphasized that the "invisible" product of their effort—their new energy, higher morale, and higher productiv-ity—was from his point of view their most valuable outcome. At the end, he threw the meeting open to questions from the audience. The first question: "The building is great! Where can we get a copy of those wonderful plans?" The audience totally missed the point. To them, the process was only a way to get a result. They didn't want to go through the process. . . only to get the result.

If there is one thing that the way of transition and the path of the life-journey teach, it is that it is that when we neglect the process and try instead to copy the outcome, we fail completely to get what we were after. Copying always creates something that is dead, because it simplifies the original and does not arise from the real creativity that is always present when real people are in an actual neutral zone.

Although the three phases of transition seem so simple as to be devoid of subtlety and life, they lead us directly to what is most unique about us and produce those self-expressed results that can be produced in no other way. We cannot *plan* our way into achieving those results, only *live* our way into them by taking on the challenges that life presents us. Like Dorothy washing the witch's kitchen floor, we achieve our breakthroughs not by setting out to break through, but by doing the work that is right in front of us.

We turn out to break through the barriers and to realize our greater potentialities, not by a willed excursion into new psychological territory, but by the willingness to view our own individual crises as critical opportunities to let go of who we have been, and to set forth on the journey toward becoming something more. Back in the seventies, many of us tried a variety of "growth" experiences, but although they were often interesting, they seldom changed us significantly because in our excitement we missed the crucial turn. We visited Oz after Oz, but never understood that renewing a worn-out life doesn't come from seeing new places but from embracing wholeheartedly the natural experience of transition.

Your transition-generated journeys will always have destinations, and after the fact those destinations may turn out to be interesting enough to make others want to retrace your steps. But they cannot do so, for those steps were taken from where you actually were right then, and that is what gave them their vitality. (Your imitators could capitalize on their own transition in the same way that you did, of course, but when they start to do so, they find a difficult ending ahead of them. That's when they decide to take the shortcut of imitation and skip the pain.) They try to turn wherever you ended up arriving into a place-to-aim-at, and then plan from Day One to arrive there. But the journey is the whole point. And besides it was *your* journey, not theirs.

The pattern we see, looking back from the journey's conclusion, is visible only from that viewpoint. It is like those iridescent colors in a fabric that can be seen only from one particular angle. A *planned journey* is an oxymoron. The apple seed has no "plan" as it grows into a tree; there is no "plan" to the changes it goes through in response to the turning seasons. It is simply *apple-ing.* The genetic coding that enables it to become what it can become is not a plan. It is simply built-in information that helps it *to apple.*

Because apples become what they are meant to become so much more naturally than we humans do, we need a metaphorical pattern, such as the journey, to tell us where we are going. It is like those homing signals that airplanes use to land, signals that don't lay out all of reality as a big map does but that simply say "a little to the left—a little further left—O.K., now, hold that—but lift your nose a bit . . ." They don't give you a big picture that enables you to stand back and say, "there I am." But they get you through the storm safely and bring you in when it is so dark that you can't see the ground.

Journeys also have the big picture quality too, of course. But that is after the fact, when we are at home by the fire looking through the snapshots: "That is when we were in Tuscany. . . and that one was taken in Wales." When we are en-route, the big-picture quality serves to help us to take ourselves a little more seriously: "I'm outward bound to. . . Paris. . . or the Grail Castle. . . or the Emerald City." They help us to define what we are putting behind us: an old life or conscription into the Czar's army or the Plagues of Egypt. We may be headed home to our Ithaca or Kansas, even though (as the man said) *you can't go home again.*

•   •   •

> *It seems as if the Deity dressed each soul which he sends into nature in certain virtues and powers not communicable to other men, and sending it to perform one more turn through the circle of beings, wrote* "Not transferable" *and* "Good for this trip only" *on these garments.*
>
> Ralph Waldo Emerson

So there aren't clear directions to follow. There have been, however, three ideas about the journey that have served me well so far, and I pass them on to you as one traveler to another.

- *First*, every journey is a round-trip that does not end when you reach your imagined destination, but only after a return trip where you bring back whatever you gained and with its help transform here into what you have been seeking.

- *Second*, the journey experience exists at every level—from that of the whole lifetime to that within every transition we make. It may even be that this "whole lifetime" is simply one of those little transitions within some larger cycle of existence.

- And *third*, it is being on the path—the way—that has the effect upon us, not the steps we take on getting to the path's destination.

No wonder planning is such a misleading concept. It takes your eyes off where you are and how your life is now, which is the essential data of existence. You fail to arrive where you *planned*, not because you couldn't visualize the place but because you didn't see that the path you were on was the place—if only you could see it at the right angle to reveal its iridescence.

eight

Discovering My Vocation

*The one predominant duty is to find one's work and to
do it.*

Charlotte Perkins Gilman

If you were advising young people on the careers they could follow,
you would suggest several logical approaches. You might talk about
finding just what it is they are good at. You would probably ask what
they wanted to get out of their work and what they most valued. You
would try to help them discover what fields were going to grow bigger in the years ahead. You might suggest that they visit and even in-
terview people who did the kinds of things they were considering as
career options. You would certainly have them talk to the counselor
at their school to find out what college major would be best for their
intended career. And then, fearing that all of these things were insuf-
ficient, you would keep passing along to them articles with titles like
"Ten Steps to a Wonderful Career."

You would do all of these things, in spite of the fact that you did
not do them yourself. You would do them, in spite of the fact that, of
all the people that you know who are presently working successfully
and happily in their vocational fields, *very few of them chose their
work by that kind of logical and systematic method.* Even most of the

career counselors who tell people to do those things *didn't, themselves, do what they advise!*

My point here doesn't concern hypocrisy. It involves the way in which we believe that life ought to be lived logically, while in fact it is actually lived according to quite different principles. And the different principles aren't bad habits that we ought to break; they are approaches that not only actually work, but that also correspond to fundamental truths about living. They would work even better if they were made explicit and practiced consciously.

Let's begin by admitting that most of us took a confusing, unmarked, cross-country route to wherever we have ended up. But we worry that if our children or other young people that we care about did that, they would (choose one)

A. Get lost and end up nowhere
B. Squander their talents—and end up nowhere
C. Fail to find a good-paying job—and end up nowhere
D. Get frustrated, take up drugs—and end up nowhere

They wouldn't, in short, have such good luck as we did—because, God knows, *we didn't know what we were doing, so we must have had a lot of luck.*

I'll have to bypass here the important child-rearing issue of letting young people make (and learn from making) their own mistakes. What I want to talk about is an extension of my earlier point about there being two *ways:* the method-way and the path-way. We usually think we are looking for the method-way, but most of what we actually end up accomplishing and benefiting from in our lives came from living and following—sometimes thoughtlessly and even in spite of ourselves—the twisting and turning route of the path-way.

We imagine that we should do with our lives what we do with the plants that we grow. Knowing that decomposing plant material and animal waste make the best fertilizer, we analyze the chemical composition of those materials, make a list of the results, and then artificially construct a synthetic substance that combines the elements in that analysis. In spite of the fact that it lacks the organic materials that rebuild the soil, attract earthworms and good insects, and add trace substances that were too much trouble to include in the chemical fertilizer, we scatter the resulting pellets and feel that we have taken care of our plants. But lives, like plants, grow from a rich mulch of decayed dreams and abortive efforts, whose effect on future growth is not duplicated by the logical 1–2–3 methods that we endorse in the advice we offer others.

When I look back over my own career, the first thing that strikes me is how much confusion and wasted effort there is, how many wrong turns I took, and how much plain dumb luck I had. The second thing that strikes me is that my own experience is about par for the course: I chose my college major, English, mainly because my father had majored in it and later taught it. If I were choosing a major today, I'd probably choose archeology or economics or music. But those subjects would have been radical departures from my programming, and back then I would have felt that I wasn't making a good decision. I would also have said that I had no interest in such majors.

When I graduated from college, I decided to get more education. If you had asked me why, I would have told you about the value of graduate study. But in retrospect I have to admit that it looks to me less like value than like fear: the fear of launching out on my own and following an unmarked trail. Academic work had all those signs and markings (called "degree requirements") and although I often complained about them, they gave me the feeling that I was doing the right thing and was on track for a career as... a... as... a teacher. Why that? I would have told you (back then) that teaching interested me. But now I'd have to admit that with a father, a mother, a grandmother and two aunts who were teachers, I was just going into the family business.

I felt that I was making a really independent decision when I decided to leave the field of English and American literature and enter a graduate program in English history at Columbia University. That may not seem like the most radical of shifts—especially since my favorite aunt was an English history professor at Rutgers University, who introduced me to her friends (who were my future professors) at Columbia. But at the time, I thought that I was heading off in a really new direction.

I never got really comfortable at Columbia or in English history, although I think now that the real issue was that I was simply tired of being in school after seventeen years. I could have left the university and just tackled some career, but I didn't know what career would be "right for me." So, after taking and passing the State Department examinations (I envisioned myself negotiating treaties and settling international disputes), I simply went limp and let myself get drafted—the draft was still in existence then.

Cruising along on automatic pilot, I entered a training program for supply clerks and came out of it fully qualified to inventory overshoes, distribute canteens and supervise the collection of laundry for the tank company to which I was assigned. I did that for a year and a half, first in Kentucky and then in Germany.

As my discharge date got closer, I was faced with the very same decision that I had been avoiding earlier. I recalled what people had said that I'd be good at, remembering that several had mentioned academic administration—did I mention that my father had been the president of a theological seminary?—and I wrote to three people that I knew who were college administrators. Two of them replied with good advice (go back to graduate school, and so forth), and one of them said that he had just become the president of a small college and was looking for a director of admissions. What luck!

Whenever I read advice about the important role that *networking* plays in career development, I think of that job offer. It came, as the advisers say most offers do, through a personal contact. But it wasn't a contact made by "networking." It was from a man whose son had been in my cabin when I was a counselor at a boy's camp one summer. I had maintained contact with the family because I liked them and because they were located about half-way between my family's home in Maine and my college in Massachusetts. I often stopped at their house and used their bathroom on my weekend trips home. Is that "networking"? If it is, it's the natural mulch-variety of networking, not the fancy 10–10–10 fertilizer type of "enhancing your network."

Most of the successful careers I have studied take their shape through actions and efforts that are the natural byproducts of ordinary living, not special things that you do for "career development." Developing a career is properly only one aspect of living a life, not a field with a life of its own. That is not to say that you shouldn't try to look for opportunities or to promote yourself or to enhance your skills. It is just that it is by seizing the opportunities that come along and following your inner voices that call on you to try *this* or to go *there* that you find the path that you identify in retrospect as "my career."

Take me. I went to Brown University for a Ph.D. because I got turned down by Harvard. And I got turned down there because they thought that I couldn't pass the foreign languages tests that you had to pass to get a doctorate in my chosen field. Brown turned out to be a wonderful place for me, but I would never have gone there if life hadn't pushed me. After graduate school, my professional friends urged me to go to a more prestigious college, but I went back to Pine Manor College, where I had begun as director of admissions. I stayed there four years, during which I taught more different courses than I ever would have taught at a big university. I had the chance to experiment with academic writing that was not so specialized as to be trivial, and I read an enormously rich mix of books, without the pressure to focus on a narrow field of study.

When I was ready to leave Pine Manor, I had three offers to consider and chose Mills because Mondi was from Northern California. (Again, it wasn't the *best place*, or even a *good way to make a decision*. But the results were great.) Mills was something like Pine Manor: lots of freedom and encouragement to try new things. I found myself developing completely new interests, some (like psychology and anthropology) totally outside my professional area.

Was it because of this growth of new interests or in spite of it that I found myself chafing at the limitations of the role of professor of literature? At first, I tried to work within the freedom I had. That was how I ended up teaching the course in autobiography that taught me so much.

Those years of the late sixties and early seventies were exciting, if troubling, times in higher education—sit-ins, student strikes and all kinds of educational experiments. I became "experimental." I tried having the students grade their own work and offered unconventional alternatives to student papers. In one of my classes on modern American poetry, two women did a topless dance while a third read poems that the three of them had written. The department chairman called me in the next day for a friendly chat about whether I was "really happy with my role as a professor of literature."

·   ·   ·

People don't choose their careers: They are engulfed by them.

John Dos Passos

I describe these stages in my career path, not to burden you with more than you want to know about the meandering vocational path that I have followed, but to give one example of how a career that most people judged to be successful—I had by then become, after all, the Aurelia Henry Reinhardt Professor of Literature at a good private college—was really a journey without an itinerary. That is not to say that I went along without plans or intentions, but only that I didn't do it the way we advise young people to. Instead of using the methods-way of career development, I let the path-way itself give me the cues I needed.

To give you a fully textured sense of what I mean by the "cues" from the path itself, I would have to go far beyond the sketchy detail I have offered here. I might tell you, for example, about first going into psychotherapy and discovering how much more profoundly that process was changing me than anything that I did in the classroom changed my students. That discovery set me to pondering how I could find a different kind of role—one that was more personal and deep than conventional subject-matter teaching but less esoteric and burdened with ideas about sickness than psychotherapy— through which I could work with people at greater depth.

I might relate my attempt to find other teachers who shared my frustrations and dreams about something better. In 1969 I went around to Stanford University and the University of California— Berkeley, as well as to Esalen Institute and other counterculture centers, and tried to talk them into putting on a summer program for college teachers who wanted to learn how to help their students "develop," not just get educated. At the time, that endeavor was called humanistic education, and it was fairly common on the elementary and secondary level, but not in higher education.

Well, everyone thought it was a Very Interesting Idea (you could hear the capitals click out of their mouths), but they were all very busy with other things. One evening, I was telling Mondi what fools they all were. She listened with interest and then said, "Why don't *you* do it?"

"Me? Myself?"

"Oh, you'd have to use Mills College, somehow," she said, as though she couldn't be bothered with spelling out the details just now. "But, yes, you. It's your idea. You know the kind of program you want. So, just produce it."

"You don't understand," I said, with a little note of panic inexplicably entering my voice. "To do something like this, you really have to. . . know what you're doing. You have to. . . know all about this kind of thing."

I'll spare you the rest of a discussion that left me both scared and excited. Suffice it to say that the next day I went to the college president and got authorized to use college buildings for a two-week faculty-development program the next summer. I called a couple of teachers at nearby institutions who were also interested in humanistic education, and one of them volunteered to help me. Within a week I had applied to the Danforth Foundation for a grant to underwrite the startup costs, and two months later a check for $25,000 arrived. A month after that, the noted psychologist, Abraham Maslow, agreed to be the keynote presenter. We sent out brochures, and thirty teachers from U.S. and Canadian colleges enrolled.

Ironically, Maslow died that spring, but even without him the First Annual [sic!] Summer Workshop in Humanistic Education for College Teachers was a stunning success. That is, it was a success and I was stunned. At least a dozen lives and careers were permanently changed by it—my own among them. I was never again able to view teaching as lifelong teachers did. Henceforth, I viewed it as something that I was currently doing while I discovered what to do next.

I spoke in a previous chapter of people who are "ripe for transition." I was ripe. Inwardly I was starting to let go of the assumptions about work that had led me into teaching and to loosen my hold on the image of myself as a literature teacher. I was looking for another path to take. After that first success, I applied for another grant, this one to fund a year of training in group process and personal growth techniques at Esalen Institute. I failed to get that grant, but in its place I undertook a self-directed learning project made up of group-experiences, training seminars and reading.

Then Jim Bugental, Maslow's last-minute replacement on the faculty of the summer institute, called one day to say that he and some of his colleagues were starting a training program for lay therapists. Did Mondi and I want to join it? I didn't even ask her before I said, "Of course." When you are on a roll, you keep moving.

•   •   •

You make what seems a simple choice: Choose a man or a job or a neighborhood—and what you have chosen is not a man or a job or a neighborhood, but a life.

Jessamyn West

You don't exactly follow a path. There isn't a path, exactly. It is more like following the contours of the land. You come to a place where the shape of the earth itself causes you to turn to the left, and another place where to cross that river you have to cut off to the right. Although there seems to be no logic to your path, being on it makes all the difference.

After that training program for lay therapists had gone on for a few months, a group of the students and a couple of the trainers started getting together for dinner after we finished our sessions. We had a good time, and before long we were talking about how wonderful it would be if we all lived closer together—so that we could see each other frequently, maybe sharing child-care and eating together a couple of times a week.

It wasn't much of a step from talking that way to actually looking (just hypothetically, at first) for property where the six families represented in our group could live side by side in a little "community." That step charged the group with the new energy of a shared purpose. Mondi and I took our three young daughters along on property-hunting trips, during which the youngest (then still in nursery school) invariably asked, "Is *this* where we're going to live?" Starting close in to the Bay Area, because we all planned to keep our jobs, we gradually ventured farther and farther out in search of acreage at a price we could afford. When we finally found the property, it was two hours north of San Francisco—too far for us to keep our jobs.

Remember this: *Whatever it is that you intend to achieve by whatever you do isn't likely to be the thing you actually accomplish by doing it.* The attraction is just the window dressing. It is the bargain specials, which do not (it turns out) come in your size. It's the bone that the burglar gives your watch-dog to keep it from barking while he takes your jewels. The actual result, the lesson or the payoff, is discovered only over time, and often in ways that you could not have known in advance. The most important results of what you do are what, in other contexts, would be called "by-products" or "side effects." If our lives were pharmaceuticals, they'd require warning labels.

In my case, we had set out to add an interesting new living situation to our lives, and what happened was that we had to discard our old lives and get completely new ones. We formed "The Community," as we rather grandly called our six-family group, and remodeled and built houses on eighty-five acres outside of Forestville, a little town on the Russian River. "How did you ever decide to do this?" friends would ask. It was hard to know where to begin, and by the time we had found the loose end of the thread of cause and reason, they were talking about something else.

•   •   •

The door into life generally opens behind us, and a hand is put forth which draws us in backwards.

George MacDonald

When we made the big jump from living near our jobs to living too far away to keep our jobs, we talked about developing some kind of collective work to support ourselves in the community. I liked gardening and keeping chickens and assumed that whatever income that our collective work generated would be used to fund a greatly simplified, more self-sufficient style of living. But the group as a whole wasn't as enamored of radical simplification as I was. (Some of them still talk, while rolling their eyes melodramatically, about the night that I served cattails from the pond as a vegetable at our comm unity dinner.) So, although we kept talking about our common work and even got so far as sketching out the kinds of retreats and seminars we would run for people who still lived a pressure-cooker life in the city, we never actually took the steps necessary to make it happen.

I felt personally cheated by this failure to come up with a common vocation, and I could work myself into quite a state laying out my case: Here, I gave up a really good teaching job with the understanding that we were going to create some way to support ourselves. . . and I thought everyone else had bought into this plan. . . and now I was the only person who kept talking about our common work! Of course, the others (including Mondi, by this time) were either psychotherapists, who were even then moving their practices to nearby Santa Rosa; or else their activities were portable—one man ran a family property-investment business and another ran a charitable foundation. There was one other guy who

had given up a regular job, but he was within a couple years of retirement, so he just retired early. And then there was me: no job, and at
forty, much too young to retire.

Friends used to visit us at the community and talk about how
brave we were to have made such a big change in our lives. I never
knew what to say. To me, it felt as though the path of my life had
suddenly taken a sharp turn, and I had gone around the corner because I didn't want to be left behind. I don't mean to say that it didn't
feel risky. It did. I awoke in the night sometimes, asking myself what
I had done. I heard from family members that my aunt—the one
who had introduced me to her English historian friends at Columbia—was worried that I wouldn't be able to get back into the teaching world when I realized (as I surely would) that I had made a
mistake. My other aunt, the head of a high school English Department, was said to be "just sick" over my decision. As if to prove their
fears well grounded, *Who's Who in America* dropped me from its
pages at the end of my first year in the community. It was an official
sign that I was nobody now.

With my former life being so firmly embedded in the family business of teaching, it felt as though I had left behind much more than a
job or a career. I thought of how few risks I had taken in my life and
of how my path had always just seemed to lead on to another stretch
of territory, and to nice territory at that. An image that kept coming
to my mind was that of "sailing off the edge of the world" a-la-
Columbus, but I dismissed it as grandiose. I felt that I had broken
some pretty important rule, however, and that I might now turn into
some kind of an outcast.

I started to work with some of the patients of my fellow-commu-
nity members who were therapists in a miniseminar called "Telling
Your Life-Story." It was the old autobiography course, untied from
its moorings as a composition course, and repositioned now as a
pure self-discovery experience. Whenever I got to the point of asking
my clients what it was time to let go of now, and what chapter of
their life was beginning at this point, I would inwardly pause to see if
any answers were peeping out of the shadows of my own mind.

I didn't spot any burning bushes, but I could see that I was gradually growing more comfortable working outside of an institution and beyond the role of an employee. I didn't have a name for what I was or what I did yet, but I knew that it involved helping people through transition, and I was starting to be able to talk about it more easily.

As a recovering teacher, I still had moments of temptation, however. One day I went to Santa Rosa Junior College, the local community college, and talked to the dean of instruction. "I want to teach a course for you," I said with what I hoped was great conviction.

"A course in what?"

"It's called *Being in Transition*," I said with the sinking feeling that the title didn't quite stack up against *The Rise of The West* or *Organic Chemistry* or *Introduction to Dental Hygiene*.

"We don't teach that course," he said with the tone of one who hoped that he wouldn't have to explain the business that *real colleges* were in. Then he took pity on me. "You might go over to the Women's Re-Entry Center. They're dealing with a lot on personal change over there—and they aren't as constrained as we are by the need to offer real courses." I thanked him and got out of his office without falling over anything.

The Women's Re-Entry Center turned out to be exactly the right place for me. Their clients—women re-entering college after years of family duties or ill-paid clerical work—were very much "in transition." They had made a change that the college told them was wonderful and that many of their friends and family made them feel was a terrible mistake. I learned there how one person's transition can put everyone within a family (or any other human system that the individual belongs to) into transition too. "It's fine for you to go off and get all that new education," one woman's husband told her when she got home late from a class. "But that don't mean that I have to give up getting my dinner cooked. . . and. . . and. . . having a *wife!*"

If it wasn't clear enough from my own experience, I quickly saw how unalterable is the rule that any successful transition must start with letting go of how things used to be—and that most *un*successful transitions start with failing to handle the ending well. And I saw that when you wanted to make a change, you seldom thought much about the endings that might be involved.

And I could see that people in transition who wanted a change to happen found it hard to feel any real sympathy for the people who lost something in the ensuing transition. I came to understand how that inability to sympathize got in the way of helping people through the transition. I also saw clearly how the failure of affected people to get through the transition could jeopardize the change itself.

The "course" at the Women's Re-Entry Center led to my own seminars under the rubric of Passage-Ways and to occasional special events in which I explored what other kinds of assistance could be offered to people in transition. My own understanding of transition and of how to help people get through it continued to grow, but it didn't take much to throw me back into a state of self-doubt and longing for a more conventional career situation.

I remember sitting on a flight to Portland, Oregon, in the mid-seventies, behind three men who worked for Northern California wineries. They talked nonstop about vintages and varietals, about the weather and the equipment used to make the wine, and about the strategy being pursued by this winery vs. that one. I envied those men so! They had a common language. They understood each other well enough to argue. They belonged to a profession and had similar problems. They had mentors and had recognizable positions in the business. Yet, at the same time, I found their conversation utterly inane. One of them bellowed, "A '70 merlot? Hell, no. A '71, maybe, or a '70 cab, but not a merlot!" And the other two nodded, as though the first one had uttered some kind of oracular truth.

·   ·   ·

Make no little plans. They have no magic to stir men's blood.

Daniel H. Burnham

It was at about this time that I decided I had not been bold enough. I got an idea for a big public program, even bigger than my

First [*But Only*] Annual Summer Workshop for College Teachers. I would invite six or eight experts each to do two hours on some particular segment of the life cycle. The program as a whole would take listeners through the whole lifetime in a single weekend, showing how each step from birth through death represented a significant developmental transition. Ira Progoff, who was well known for his use of personal journals as a self-exploration tools, agreed to do an overview of the life-journey. I convinced the seventy-five-year-old Carl Rogers to talk about the developmental aspects of old age— something he had never done in public before. I found other speakers to talk about childhood and youth. And the celebrated Elizabeth Kübler-Ross said she would do two hours on dying as a developmental experience.

I myself took the developmental aspects of midlife. (Later, I wondered if I weren't a little like someone who buys a baseball team so that he can play shortstop.) I certainly wasn't in the league of my well-known fellow-presenters, but I was so excited by what I was creating that I didn't worry about that.

I had no idea how many people would come, but I decided that it was better to aim high. So I rented the Marin Civic Center, the 2,000-seat auditorium that was one of Frank Lloyd Wright's final projects. I worked out a cosponsorship arrangement with the Association for Humanistic Psychology, and began beating the bushes for enrollments. Well, the enrollments came in beyond anything I had expected, and on the eve of the event more than 1,700 people had signed up.

Then the night before the conference started, I got a call from Kübler-Ross's assistant, saying that my star attraction had pneumonia and was going to have to pull out. The assistant was arranging to have an associate fly out from Boston to speak in her place. But the person wasn't famous, and a good half of the attendees had been drawn by Kübler-Ross's presence.

I knew just how Icarus had felt when his wings started to soften in the sunshine. I reworked the schedule for the event and wrote up some additional things to say. But my mind was full of images of people walking out by the hundreds, and I was feeling just awful. Then the phone rang. A pleasant voice asked if I were Bill, then said that he had heard that Elizabeth had "stood me up" and offered to help. He said that his name was Ram Dass.

The program went off just beautifully. Ram Dass, not so well known then as he has since become, was wonderful. Everyone was good. The audience loved it. And I had done it myself, persevering in spite of people having warned me that it was taking a big risk. Well, there! Watch me now! My career was really going to take off!

In fact, the heavens did not open, and invitations to speak for huge fees did not roll in. I found myself back doing the things I had been doing before my huge success. In a way, nothing had changed. I still had to sit down and decide what to do next. But in another way, everything had changed. I had learned that the biggest project I could have imagined happened just as little projects do: starting with an idea, assembling the resources to get it launched and working like hell. Never again would I rule out any path as impossible.

I had put together a little self-published paperback on adult development and transition called *The Seasons of Our Lives* (1977)[1], and had sold it at the conference. True to my argument that nothing happens for the reason you intend, I had started the manuscript and written the first half of it during a week that I spent marooned in Vernal, Utah, waiting for a kidney stone to make up its mind whether or not to pass. I got the pamphlet printed at a local copy-shop and sold 3,000 copies in the next several years. More important, it convinced me that I could use writing to get my ideas out and establish myself as a person with something to say.

• • •

No man is born into the world whose work
Is not born with him; there is always work,
And tools to work withal, for those who will.

James Russell Lowell

I have already noted that I never intended to work in organizations. My background and personal values were so individually oriented that I was very slow to appreciate the critical role that organizations play in modern society and in our economy. But when *Transitions* (1980) led to invitations to speak to groups of managers, I accepted. And within five years, I had shifted the focus of my work from individuals to organizations.

From the beginning, I loved the experience of going into a new organization and learning all about it. My first three clients were the U.S. Forest Service, KalKan Foods and McDonnell-Douglas Astronautics: I couldn't have covered much more ground than that: Douglas firs, dog food and the Space Lab. I was back to being a student, and every organizational visit was the meeting of a wonderful free seminar that I was taking! I couldn't have been much more ignorant when I began, though. I can still remember the moment I made the wise decision not to ask what "CEO" stood for; I just said I was pleased to meet the man.

I worked with those organizations on managing the disruptive "transition process" that got triggered off by every change they put people through. I could show that the transition could make a change unmanageable, and that the money spent on getting people through it successfully was a tiny fraction of what they would lose if the people didn't make the transition and the change went badly.

Some of the organizations that were most interested in transition-management were companies, like Intel, that put their people through enormous amounts of change and did so constantly. (One of the jokes at that Silicon Valley company was, "If my manager calls, find out his name, will you?") The company built transition-management into the training program that all its managers were sent through, and I trained more than 200 people at Intel to run my seminars within the company.

While I was working there, I started to realize that Intel employees didn't talk about their *jobs* the way people did at other companies where I worked. They talked about their *assignments*. At first I thought that this was just part of the jargon that any organization develops, but gradually it dawned on me that in a very real sense people at Intel didn't have regular jobs. They did something for a while and, then, did something else. They often worked on two or three project teams at once. No one resisted a new assignment because "that's not my job," and people didn't fight against reorganizations to protect their jobs either. The result was that Intel was remarkably flexible and could regroup to tackle new problems and emerging issues very quickly.

I was slow to recognize the implications of what I was seeing, but by 1990 I understood that what Intel had done was largely to "de-job" its work processes—to get work done in ways that did not require exclusive, long-term assignment of different kinds of work to different kinds of people. As my work took me elsewhere in Silicon Valley, I saw that a number of other high-tech companies were doing the same thing. Everywhere the result was the same: greater speed, more flexibility, less of a status-quo to get in the way of innovation.

All of this seemed to me to be nothing more than a way that a few organizations were restructuring their workplaces until, one day, I looked up the word *job* in the old fifteen-volume *Oxford English Dictionary* that I had inherited from my father. The word was old, going back to a Celtic root that apparently meant (like the related word "gob") "a hunk of something." Fairly early it had come to mean a piece of work, and by the 18th century people were talking about a "job-man" to refer to someone hired to do a particular task. (Ironically, the job-man was what today we'd call a *temp.*) It wasn't until the industrial revolution brought in the factory (and the division of labor) that people stopped talking about *doing a job* and started talking about *having a job.*"

That was an enormous change, which I started calling the first great "job-shift." With that change came all sorts of other things. As people became more mobile and communities became looser, people got their identities from the jobs they held. As less and less opportunity to work existed outside the boundaries of "jobs," people began to view their jobs as possessions. Organizations began to build their hiring, evaluation, paying, and training around jobs. The task of supervision was redefined as seeing that *people did their jobs*. Public policy was reframed on the plan of insuring that everyone could *find a good job*. We became a *job-based* economy and a *job-oriented* society.

By the time I published *JobShift* in 1994 and *Creating You & Co.* in 1997, I was ready to change my whole work-life away from helping organizations to get through whatever transition they were currently in to helping them deal effectively with the widespread de-jobbing of work that I saw going on everywhere. And I do mean "everywhere." Unlike my books on transitions, which took fifteen years to get published overseas and then went international very slowly, *JobShift* was translated into eight languages within two years. When I spoke on the topic in Europe and South America and Australia, people recognized all the symptoms.

But whereas the subject of transition was noncontroversial, talking about the job shift generated powerful feelings. Workers didn't want to hear that the jobs, which they viewed as part of God's natural order, were actually a societal creation—and, worse yet, that their jobs fitted the kind of work done in the industrial age much better than they fitted the work that was going to be done in the information age. They didn't want to hear that jobs were threatened, not just by overseas competition, the greed of executives, or the short-term fluctuations of the economy, but by a permanent shift in the work that needed doing—a shift that made the traditional job as outmoded as an oxbow.

I was excited to be caught up in controversy, especially on such a critical issue involving the well-being of so many people. However, I was startled by the depth of the hostility I encountered from some people who disagreed with me. A caller on a California talk show asked if I were a communist and then said he wanted me to know that he carried a gun, "An' I'm not scared of using it either!" A Canadian labor leader jabbed me with belligerent questions during a speech I gave in Halifax, then afterwards told me privately that he agreed with my analysis but that "Our members would vote us out if we agreed with you publicly." After an excerpt from *JobShift* appeared in *Fortune,* a letter by one of the magazine's readers dismissed my argument out of hand by saying that "American workers would never stand for it!"

Yet at the same time the daily press continued to be full of stories about further rounds of down-sizing, even by companies that were doing well financially. And the business of temporary agencies continued to grow. And *Fast Company* became an overnight sensation in the magazine world with an issue called "The Free-Agent Nation." And every survey showed that workers remained very anxious about their prospects for future employment, despite the fact that the U.S. unemployment rate was at its lowest point in decades.

It was obvious that the job-shift had created a very profound transition in which large numbers of people in all developed and most developing countries were being forced to let go of the conditions and rules that they had known and were being plunged headlong into a neutral zone that was frightening to them. It seemed to me that this subject was so important that shortly everyone would recognize it. I had left transition behind.

Within a year, however, Mondi was struggling with cancer, and I found myself brought back face-to-face with transitions again. Not just back to my old subject of organizational transition, but back to my original subject of personal transition. Yet there was a sort of poetic justice in my evolving subject matter: Journeys, unlike point-to-point trips, have a way of doubling back on themselves so that you find yourself dealing again and at another level with issues you thought that you had left behind.

•   •   •

When you truly possess all you have been and done,
which may take some time, you are fierce with reality.

Florida Scott-Maxwell

I feel as though I am back where I started in the 1970s, because I find that in the aftermath of Mondi's death and my own bereavement, individuals are more interesting to me than organizations are. It is not that corporate and governmental events are not critically important to everyone's well-being or that my own future is not intimately dependent on what happens in that world. It is just that my imagination is again captured and stirred by the experiences of individuals in ways that it was not during those years when I focused my attention on organizations.

Today, it is the way in which my own transitions bring me new challenges that excites me. It is how a deep personal loss, one that I fought every step of the way, has opened up areas for creative insight and spiritual growth. It is how new meanings are disclosed to me as I retell the simple narrative of my own career. It is how that the most fixed and completed of things, *the past*, is really alive and growing; and how as the past changes, it creates the possibility of a new future. I find myself wanting to help individuals to understand the value that resides in the story of their lives and the transitions they have gone through.

I believe especially that a person's quest for a vocation is rich with meaning. At one level, the story of one's work-life is no more than one of many biographical strands that make up the fabric of the whole life. But at another level, the vocational journey is for many people the core thread around which the others are wrapped. Not "vocational" in the narrow sense of a job-history, but in the widest sense of the various ways in which people are *called* by their lives to contribute to the task of doing the world's work.

The path leading me to meaningful work and a way to make a living from it has been a long and twisting one. What looked at the time like setbacks or defeats look to me now more like switchbacks that enabled me to gain altitude. What I thought I had left behind showed up again ahead of me in my path. (I was, at one point, sure that I had finished, for good, with teaching!) The points at which I had bogged down or lost the path turned out to be the hidden entrances to neutral zones that I needed to visit in order to reorient myself for the next part of my journey. The very things that I had thought were essential to my success turned out the be the baggage I needed to let go of if I were to make it over the rough ground that I had to cover in the next chapter of my life.

So. . . how has it been with you? Has your path followed a similar meander as it responded to the perpendicular force of circumstance and fortune? You might want to take a little time right now to think back over the path you have been following. You might want to look back at the chapter titles you chose back in Chapter Five. Remember that Emerson passage I quoted earlier about life being a hiero-glyphic? See if you can crack your own life's code.

nine

Finding Myself in the Neutral Zone

It's not so much that we're afraid of change or so in love with the old ways, but it's that place in between that we fear. . . It's like being in between trapezes. It's Linus when his blanket is in the dryer. There's nothing to hold on to.

Marilyn Ferguson

The neutral zone is the second of transition's three phases. It's that in-between time, after you've let go of your old life and before you have fully discovered and incorporated your new life. The ending and the new beginning are states that are characterized by doing something (*letting go* and *making a new beginning*), but the neutral zone is a time when it may seem that nothing is happening. While the other two phases of transition are often bracketed by events, the neutral zone is more like an uneventful gap in your lifetime. It is a colorless streak of emptiness that spreads across your life, like the gray smear left by a dirty eraser.

In the days that followed Mondi's death, I kept waiting for something to happen. Events took place, of course. There was the gathering of friends and family for her memorial service: my brother and my niece; an old friend who lived in Maine now; a cousin of Mondi's from Oregon; many of Mondi's friends from the Jung Institute. We held the service up in Forestville, near the house where she and I had lived for eleven years. That was the only place our family had really put down roots. When it was over, my children and I—I probably said *our* children at the time, not yet being used to speaking in the singular—returned to the house in Mill Valley, which was still torn up in the remodel. A day later we all said good-bye, and everyone went home. I stayed and waited for my life to start up again.

•   •   •

Corn grows in the night.

Henry David Thoreau

It is difficult to describe the neutral zone without speaking metaphorically. It is a season of dormancy when life withdraws back into the root to get ready for a long, cold season without whatever had given warmth and meaning to life-before-the-ending. It is a strange no-man's-land between one world and the next. It is a zone where you pick up mixed signals, some coming from the past and some from the future. Sometimes the signals jumble into noise, while at other times they cancel each other out, leaving only an eerie silence. It is a low-pressure area, where all kinds of heavy weather is drawn into the vacuum left by the loss. It is a dark night of the heart—or, maybe, a long dark twilight that refuses to resolve itself into either real day or true night.

As I ate breakfast the morning after everyone had left, I realized that it felt as though I had been in the neutral zone for ages and ages. Time slows down greatly in the neutral zone. The days now seemed to be forty hours long. And yet at the same time, weeks had a way of disintegrating, leaving behind only a few remembered moments.

I found myself in a situation where, for the first time in almost forty years, I could do anything I wanted to do. But as far as I could tell, there was absolutely nothing that I wanted to do. I often caught myself staring at the wall, my mind a blank, with Mondi's illness and death seeming like a dream from which I might at any moment wake. But then I would think back to our life together before the cancer started colonizing her body, and that life—how innocent and untroubled it looked in retrospect—*that life* was the dream and her death the waking.

Part of the confusion was that there were two linked transitions occurring, and the result was a kind of double-dipping into the neutral zone. The first transition had been triggered off by her original diagnosis, and it started when her life as a normal healthy woman came to an end. In that transition, the letting-go had been slow and gradual, punctuated by periods when we hoped that the cancer would prove to be treatable. In that first transition, the neutral zone was an underlying state of painful uncertainty which was always there, waiting to be activated by negative test results or the discovery of a new symptom. But although these trigger events were powerful setbacks, they were never definitive. The test numbers went down, but then they came back up—before heading lower again. And their ultimate significance was always in doubt. Everything was ambiguous.

"What does the liquid in the lung mean?" we'd ask the doctor. "Well, it could be from where we went in to drain the lung before, a more or less benign build-up, or it could be that the cancer has spread to the lung."

"How can we find out which it is?"

"We can draw some of the fluid, and look to see if it has cancer cells in it."

"And if it doesn't. . . ?"

"Well, unfortunately that wouldn't really be conclusive either, because the cells might be in the tissue but not in the fluid."

"So, then you'd biopsy the tissue?"

"We could, but we don't want to burden the lungs any more than we have to. Besides, it wouldn't really make much difference. The treatment would be the same either way."

It wouldn't make much difference whether the cancer had spread to her lungs or not! Just life or death! But to find out which, we'd have to operate again, and that might tip the scales toward death. So we wouldn't do it. So we'd just wait and see, wondering which way it would go. Wondering. The name of this game was Living with Uncertainty.

Some of our friends urged her to be hopeful and positive. Belief, they said, was a critical factor in healing. She must think that she was going to get well, that she *was* getting well. She had to keep visualizing her immune system rising up like a native army and destroying the imperialistic cancer.

By that time, I was in a mood to do unquestioningly anything that might help. But Mondi was more discriminating. She tried to visualize the good little troops of her immune system killing the invaders. But then, one day, she announced that the battle metaphor didn't work for her. "I just can't get over the feeling that the cancer is *me* too, *me against me* or something. So, now I'm negotiating with them." The deal was that they'd have to stay in a walled compound and stop attacking the locals. It sounded weird, but then her test results showed an improvement, so maybe it was a good idea.

As I said in the first chapter, she ended up deciding that "you just don't know" and that both optimism and pessimism were the fantasies that we use to escape from the awful uncertainty. I myself could sympathize with both the optimists and the pessimists, but like her, I came to the point of being an agnostic about outcomes. We tried to take the days—and the news they brought—as they came. You couldn't deal in larger units of time in that neutral zone. Time was like the manna that Moses found in his neutral zone: good for that day only. We spent that first neutral zone, the time between the diagnosis and the beginning of her dying, taking existence day by day like a couple of initiates on a terminal walkabout.

·   ·   ·

Even cowards can endure hardship;
only the brave can endure suspense.

Mignon McLaughlin

That was the first neutral zone. The second one started when I was alone. The ending had been unequivocal this time: Death reduces the ambiguity to zero. But once again, I was living with uncertainty. The first time it had been uncertainty about which of two knowable ways things would turn out. This time there were no futures at all, nothing to hope for, nothing to fear. Life seemed to have come to a standstill, though all around me I could see others rushing about with an almost manic energy. But they were part of some parallel universe, visible but inaccessible to me.

Being around most other people was difficult at this time, for in almost everything they said there was the unspoken subtext: "Are you feeling better? I hope that you're feeling better. Please say that you're feeling better." Their concern for me was genuine, but there were few of them who could resist the temptation to urge on me a less unhappy and discouraged view of things. "Well, of course you're having a hard time," they'd say. "Mondi's been dead less than a month. You need time." Which was true, of course, but it was also their way of *saying something*, when what I was discovering that I preferred was silence.

On the other hand, I was drawn to people who were discouraged and unsure of themselves. I went to a touring exhibit of classical Chinese art during this time, and I saw there a scroll that attracted me mightily. I liked it partly for the scene it showed of an elderly man alone in the mountains. (One of my fantasies was to go away for and live by myself in the Sierras.) But it also attracted me because of the poem had been written to accompany the picture. I felt as though the words had been drawn forth from my own mind:

> I have seen the waters of the Yellow River
> Changing endlessly from muddy to clear.
> The current rushes forward, fast as an arrow;
> I am buffeted by life like a drifting reed.

And then the lines that chilled me with recognition: "After countless cycles of calamity,/Still no enlightenment comes."[1]

Still no enlightenment. In the passage rituals that I had studied, people received messages from the gods or the ancestors. In the three-day vigil in Eureka Valley that I myself had kept when I turned fifty, I had heard owls calling all night, so persistently and close to me that the shaman who conducted my sweat-lodge ceremony after I returned told me that I had surely encountered my own totem animal. But in the mundane vigil I kept during those first days alone, there were no messages whatsoever.

The earlier neutral zone, while we were waiting to learn what the cancer was going to do, now seemed almost exciting by contrast. There had been things happening then. There was a future to be anticipated or dreaded, depending on the week's news. In spite of our agnosticism about outcomes, there was still a sense that you could make something happen if you found the right door to open. This time, however, the uncertainty was over whether there were any doors at all. Maybe life hadn't turned into a great doorless wall.

Everything had stopped. Not tasks, of course, for the days were full of calls and letters about the personal and legal issues surrounding Mondi's death. Those were endless, but at the end of such days I'd find myself staring out the window into deep space, feeling as alone as though I were on some solitary interstellar journey.

Would I work again? At sixty-three, I was old enough to stop if I lived simply. I read about college classmates who had retired. They sounded happy. I couldn't decide what I wanted. I couldn't even imagine how to decide. Or, on another tack: Would I find another woman and begin a new serious relationship—not marriage, maybe, but being a couple? That possibility was like wondering if I might walk across the sea to Europe. I could imagine the destination, but getting there was just didn't seem possible. I hadn't started up a relationship from scratch for almost forty years.

The uncertainty about my future slowly began to disclose an unexpectedly meaningful quality as the weeks went by. Embracing that uncertainty willingly began to seem like a strange sort of a spiritual discipline. When I felt uncertain and anxious, I could watch my mind start to produce pseudorealities to calm me. It was like the pe-

riod before Mondi died, when my mind busily invented *interpreta-*
tions of Mondi's test results. Now, I'd catch myself inventing imagined futures. They were mildly comforting, but they always left me
discouraged because they offered no path to follow. They were like
panoramas painted on a wall that went nowhere.

But then I'd think, "There I go again," and in my self-recognition
as a person using an imaginary future to quiet my fear, I'd see how
much of my life was spent doing that. That was a spiritual discovery
of sorts, I decided, and when I caught myself doing that, I'd say to
myself almost as if I were talking to a small child: "That's O.K., you'll
be all right; you don't have to make-believe." And, unaccountably, I'd
feel better, stronger. As the weeks went by I found that I was developing, without any systematic effort, what the British poet John Keats
called *negative capability*: being able to live with "uncertainties, mys-
teries, doubts without any irritable reaching after fact and reason."[2]

When Mondi had been alive, there had always been an imaginary
other life going on inside of me. Even though I was scarcely aware of
it, I was always imagining how I would live if I didn't have *this* life to
deal with. My imaginary life was made up of the places I'd go, the
new people I'd meet, the unfamiliar things I'd try—if I were free to
do so. Looking at the TV schedule. . . I'd think: I'd watch that movie
if I weren't already "taken" for the afternoon by Mondi. Reading the
travel section in the Sunday paper, I'd think, if I lived alone I could
just drop everything and go to New York. I'd check out the nearby
movies, the symphony schedule, an article about an author talking at
a local bookstore, even though I knew that there wasn't much chance
I'd attend any of these events.

Now, in my solitary neutral zone, all of these things were really
possible. It was as though life were taunting me: "OK, big boy. You've
said that this is what you'd do if you didn't have these responsibili-
ties, distractions, demands on your time. Now . . . here's your
chance." It was exciting, in an abstract sort of a way. But because it
was just *possible*—because it didn't emanate from any powerful desire on my part—the possibilities simply tired me out and left me
feeling only more empty and purposeless.

How do you activate the creative side of the neutral zone, I wondered? How do you discover in it the "creative chaos" that I had talked about for twenty years? I thought of going to some sacred site—to Chartres, Stonehenge, Sedona—one of those power spots where spiritual presences were said to be there for the picking. I did go to England, to give a speech, and my British publisher told me about the wonderful ruined twelfth-century abbey at Llanthony, in the mountains of Wales. Visiting it was a wonderfully evocative experience, but I returned as full of confusion as I left.

•   •   •

[I]f there is a sin against life, it consists perhaps not so much in despairing of life as in hoping for another life and in eluding the implacable grandeur of this life.

Albert Camus

The world I came back to was not only lonely and gray. It also felt two-dimensional, like canvas scenery. Something that Michael Novak had written about institutions was turning out to be true of relationships as well. They exist, he said, "not merely to satisfy pragmatic needs and desires. Much more fundamentally, they function to construct and secure a sense of reality."[3] Right! With Mondi's death and the end of that relationship, I had lost more than the life we had together. I had also lost my everyday world and the sense of reality that I felt from being a part of it.

I thought back to previous turning points in my life. Getting my first job, meeting Mondi, joining the community, writing *Transitions,* starting to work in organizations: All of them occurred at a point where I had followed some path as far as I could. At such a time, I collided with some event that bumped me off the route I had been following. Each of these new beginnings had occurred when I was discouraged over not knowing which way to go. They all happened when something that I had counted on had disappeared. They all took place when I was in the neutral zone.

Each time I had found myself there, I had thought, "You are completely lost! *Now* you've done it!" But each time, in some totally unforeseeable way that seemed not only illogical but also so peculiar to that particular situation that it certainly was no sort of a guideline for the future, I had found a path right under my feet. It was always like those children's stories in which a magic door is discovered behind the clothes hanging in the closet. (Had it always been there? Why hadn't I seen in before?)

Each time it had happened in my life, I had thought of it as a one-time piece of luck. Yet even though I understood that it was unrepeatable, I also always struggled to remember afterward just what I had done to get through the place where I was stuck. I kept trying to identify the "trick" so that I could use it the next time I was stuck and so could avoid the terrible feeling of being desolate and confused. But, of course, I never figured out the trick. The good news was that I knew that I had been in this place and remembered that it had been the prelude to a new life in the past. The bad news was that I was still trying to figure out some trick to convert the uncertainty into opportunity.

"So here you are again," I was thinking one day as I was shopping for vegetables at the local Whole Foods Market. The carrots, leeks and bok choy glistened under the mist machines like holy artifacts in some temple. The self-confident matter-of-factness of the other shoppers was disconcerting, given that I was working hard to think of this—and everything I saw those days—as the possible setting for the birth of my new life. The other shoppers were apparently unaware of how accessible the enormous reality of death and rebirth was right there, right then. I oscillated between a feeling of excitement over a new life that might be just over beyond the potatoes, and a deep despair at the emptiness I felt when I realized that these were just vegetables and that I was getting carried away with all this mumbo-jumbo about death and rebirth.

•   •   •

All would live long, but none would be old.

Benjamin Franklin

Every aspect of my life was up for grabs. I didn't know what kind of work I wanted to do or even if I wanted to keep working. I liked where I was living, but I found myself imagining moving to an island off the coast of Maine. I thought about how I might meet someone that I could go out with. I did things with friends and members of my family. I went out to dinner and to plays and concerts by myself, and I imagined that I might bump into someone that I'd want to date. But I didn't. I knew a couple who had met through an ad in the Personals section of the local paper, and I read that section regularly now. But I didn't have any idea what I'd say.

"Vital older man. . . "

No, wait. Older. . . than what? It would be better to say, "63 year old man . . ." Or does that sound too old?

"Man in early sixties . . ." Is sixty-three early or middle?

I decided that "older" was vague without being inaccurate. "Vital older man seeking. . . seeking. . . "

Seeking what? A new relationship? Company? A lifelong companion? Sex? A new life? Yes, seeking a new life. But you can't advertise for a new life.

So. "Vital older man seeking a new relationship. Likes travel, intimacy, cultural events . . ." Ugh!

I couldn't imagine printing the ad—even if I could have decided what it would say—because I couldn't imagine wanting to be with anyone who would answer it. And back I went into imagining meeting a new person, while berating myself for not having done anything to make that happen.

Being older (or "older") began to prey on my mind. Alone, I felt much older than I had ever felt when Mondi was alive. As one of a couple, I had thought very little about how I could be experienced by people who didn't know me. But when I heard a friend describe someone my age as "an old guy," I cringed. It felt as though I was at the point where I ought to be thinking about winding down, rather than starting new things.

Seeking reassurance, I started noticing examples of people who did new and impressive things when they were. . . older. [4] Michelangelo had been the chief architect of St. Peter's Basilica when he was between the ages of seventy-one and eighty-nine. Claude Monet didn't even start his great series of water lilies paintings until he was seventy-three. Grandma Moses took up painting when she was seventy-eight. Marian Hart, who didn't learn to fly until she was in her fifties, flew solo across the Atlantic when she was eighty-four.

Edith Hamilton, whose books on mythology I had read with such pleasure, had not even started writing on that subject until after she retired as a school principal at sixty-five. She had not visited her beloved Athens until she was in her eighties! At ninety, when she was planning another trip, someone said that it was wonderful that she could take one last trip. "Last, hummmph!" She replied. She took *three more trips* to the classical world before she died at ninety-five. I picked up such stories like burrs. But I didn't feel very reassured by these people. I wasn't in their league. They must have known something that I didn't. And they had more initiative than I did. I didn't act—I just imagined.

One day I was in the Whole Foods Market again, studying the women who were picking over the peaches and sniffing the basil. The ones who were attractive looked so *unavailable*, and the interested ones looked so oppressively *needy* and overwhelmingly *neurotic*. I tried chatting with them—something along the lines of "The melons look good today, don't they?" But that sounded so stilted and forced that it made me want to hide my face.

In spite of knowing better, I found myself once again imagining that there was a method, a trick to breaking through the neutral-zone impasse. In my past creative breakthroughs, I had just been lucky, I decided. This time, I'd just have to pick up my fresh produce—which was, after all, what I had come for—and go home and cook up a good dinner, which I'd eat alone. Lots of people had lived fine and valuable lives alone. Lots.

A voice broke in on my reveries: "Hi. Bill. It's Susan Mitchell." I was confused and disoriented, the way you are when the external world is utterly discontinuous with your inner world. But of course I remembered her. We had worked together on a project almost ten years before. Yes, indeed. I remembered her.

She said that she had heard that my wife had died and that she was really sorry. I said something. She said something. We agreed that it was nice to bump into each other like that. She now lived in Mill Valley.

She looked wonderful. She was so friendly and warm. A huge smile. "How are you doing, Bill?"

"O.K., I guess. I'm making it. Thanks for asking."

"If you ever want to, just, talk—get together for coffee or something—give me a call."

"Thanks. I'll remember. Thanks."

We exclaimed at how we both shopped at the same market and had never seen each other there. Amazing. But now maybe we'd cross paths again. We said good-bye.

"Nice to see you." Then she was gone. And I was left trying to think what I should have said.

I felt like Parsifal, the knight of the Grail Legend, who had been told that he would find the Grail Castle and that when he finally saw the long-sought Holy Grail, he must ask, "Whom does the Grail serve?" So there he was, later, sitting in the dining hall of a castle, when suddenly the Holy Grail floated into the room and moved slowly past him. And his question? He was too amazed to speak.

There it was, so close that he could touch the thing he had spent years looking for. And his mind went blank; he was speechless. By the time he remembered the magic question that he was supposed to ask, the Grail had floated out of the room again, and he had to start his long, long quest all over again. I was even worse than Parsifal, for even when she was gone, I couldn't think what I should have said.

I decided to call her, but there was no "Mitchell, *Susan*" in the phone book—only "Mitchell, S.," and there were several of those. I put the phone book away. Later I took it out and checked again, and there were *still* no Susan Mitchells. I chose a *Mitchell, S* at random and dialed. I was terrified. My hand was so sweaty that the phone was hard to hold. It rang. And rang. Then I got an answering machine. I couldn't even tell if it was Susan's voice or not, so I launched into a hopelessly detailed and utterly irrelevant account of why I didn't know if this was *Susan* or not. But if it was, well, she had said to call if I wanted to get together and talk. And I did. Wanted to talk, that is. So. So, how about getting together for coffee? At the Book Depot Café? For coffee? We could talk. How about late tomorrow afternoon?

I hung up, relieved to be done, but ashamed at how utterly inept I had been and how stupid I had sounded. I called another *Mitchell, S.* and went through the whole routine again before I realized that the voice on the answering machine had sounded the same as the one at the previous number. I got through the experience, but I hated how afraid it made me. Well, I was out of practice. I'd been out of that business for decades. Which reminded me of how old I was. She was a lot younger, fifteen years at least. I wondered whether I came across as a fumbling elderly man. I felt embarrassed and miserable. And elderly.

She called back within a few hours. Both numbers had been hers—one home, one work—so she had heard my invitation twice. Before I had a chance to think how much worse two hearings might have been than one, she said that she would be at the Book Depot Café tomorrow at 4:00. I said, Fine. We hung up. I vowed to improve my phone skills—my social skills, generally—since I was likely to be doing things like this for some time. And, hey, I couldn't count on the next woman being an old friend who spotted me at the market. Lightning couldn't be expected to strike the same spot twice. I'd have to find other ways to meet people.

•   •   •

I felt it shelter to speak to you.

Emily Dickinson (letter)

The café was crowded, and we were squeezed in at a little round table between two bigger groups of people. To get started and in the name of updating each other on what we'd been doing in the ten years since we'd last talked, we each ran through a quick summary of our recent lives. The summaries turned imperceptibly into life-stories, and before long we were comparing notes on what it felt like to be alive. The talk went on and on, taking unexpected and wonderful turns. Suddenly it was 5:30 and she had to go. We got up, bumped into each other and laughed. Then I gave her a hug. And I kissed her. *Molester strikes. Rapist on the loose.* She looked startled but smiled. We agreed that we'd have to talk again. (I *would* have to improve my social skills. I couldn't count on my next date being such a tolerant woman.) I walked out of the café feeling happier than I had felt in a long time. We had talked so freely. It had been so interesting.

I wanted to call her immediately and set up another get-together, but I restrained myself overnight. Then I called and said I'd like to take her out to dinner. We agreed on a week from Saturday. We'd meet at the restaurant. (It didn't occur to me that that might be her way of assuring that she had the freedom of having her own car, in case I turned out to be as inept as I seemed.) The week rushed by. I was nervous but excited and hopeful.

The dinner was a disaster. Actually, the dinner was fine. *I* was the disaster. The conversation didn't flow as it had over coffee. I groped after things to talk about. She said, later, that she pretty much decided on that night that I wasn't ready for another relationship. The whole task of making connections with a new person made me so uncomfortable that I just didn't know what to say. After I said goodnight to her at her car, I decided that I had destroyed any chances I might have had.

But then the next day, there I was calling her again. This calling stuff was getting easier. During dinner the night before, we had found that we both liked to hike. As the dinner was sliding uncomfortably over the brink, we commented that it might be nice to do some activity together sometime—that is, not sit and just talk about how hard it was to talk. So I called and suggested we take a hike the next weekend. She paused perceptibly before she replied, but then in a what-the-hell tone of voice, she said, "Sure, that'd be fun." Which is how we hiked the Dipsea Trail over Mount Tamalpais to the ocean at Stinson Beach.

Defusing the intensity of being together by hiking turned out to be a great idea. We relaxed again. We learned more about each other. I learned that she had almost got married a couple of years earlier and that plans had been broken off painfully. I talked about how hard it had been to come to terms with the fact that Mondi was going to die. It was obvious that we were both worried about whether we were ready yet for another relationship.

After the downhill part of the hike, we had a wonderful breakfast in a little restaurant down at Stinson Beach and then hiked back up the mountain to where we had left my car. When we were three quarters of the way up to the parking area, I began to feel a strange sense of familiarity with the area we were hiking through. Then, suddenly, we were crossing a little trail, and I realized that we were within a hundred yards of the spot where I had scattered Mondi's ashes. I had never approached the area from below before, so I hadn't known where I was. What did this coincidence mean? Was Mondi watching? What did she think of my being with another woman—or of my ineptitude.

• • •

The world fears a new experience more than it fears anything.
Because a new experience displaces so many old
experiences. . . The world doesn't fear a new idea. It can pigeon-
hole any idea. But it can't pigeon-hole a real new experience.

D. H. Lawrence

Over the next few weeks, Susan and I saw a lot of each other and just as unexpectedly as it began, our relationship took on a life of its own. We stopped talking in a way that was so overtly meant to get to know one another and started just enjoying ourselves. Without talking about it, we started to assume after each time we were together that there would be another time together soon. I began telling people that I was dating, though I'm sure I made it sound as though it was a few dates, now and then, with several different people. My three daughters sounded ambivalent when they heard about my new activity, but said they were pleased. Susan's mother came up for a visit, and Susan brought her by my house to say hello.

At Christmas she went off to spend the holiday with friends, while I put on a big dinner for my daughters and their families. But at different times during that holiday week, I arranged for each of them to meet her. Anne was matter-of-fact about it, but sounded mildly positive. Sarah was very interested and spent time asking her questions. Margaret was polite but clearly uncomfortable with this turn of events. Later, Margaret talked about its being very hard to see me with someone besides her mother. I reminded her that this was just dating—I wasn't getting married. She said that she knew that, but it was still hard.

During that winter, Susan and I spent a lot of time together. We went out every weekend. On weeknights, one of us sometimes cooked dinner for the other after a long day of work. At my house, we'd pull up easy chairs up in front of the living room fireplace and eat on trays, while at her house we'd eat by candlelight at the table in the dining nook. We went to the symphony. We went down to Big Sur for a weekend. And we talked and talked.

We were talking on the telephone one night, just before going to sleep, when without any warning I began to shiver. I was lying in bed, so I mounded the covers over me and waited for it to pass. Finally, I told her what was going on. "I thought your voice sounded shaky," she said. "Are you getting sick?"

"No." I worked to get up courage to say what I thought was going on. "I think I'm scared," I blurted out. The minute I said it, I knew it was true.

"Of what?" she asked.

I said I didn't know. But I did. I was scared of how quickly the new life that I imagined was actually taking shape. I felt as though I had only meant to explore a new path for a little way, going just far enough down it to see what being with a new person felt like after all these years. But "a little way" was turning out to be farther and farther, and now it felt as though there was no turning back. I was really starting to love this woman. I was swept away by her sense of humor, her intelligence, her beauty, and her sweetness.

But there were a couple of problems, and the more drawn to her I was, the more I worried about them. One was timing. It felt subjectively as though it had been an eternity since Mondi's death, but actually it had not quite been a year. I knew all about how important it was to allow enough time to make a real ending and go through the neutral zone. I had even written that people who don't do that often abort the transition they are in. At best, they have to let go all over again; and at worst, they mess up their lives (and their partner's) miserably. But just *how long* was "enough," I didn't know. In the back of my mind, I kept hearing the phrase, "No big decisions for a year." That seemed arbitrary, but I was looking desperately for guidelines. "Not for a year" was better than nothing.

The second issue was our age difference. I was eighteen years older than she was. I had been in college when she was born. Again, I wished that there were guidelines to follow—although I suspected that if there had been, I'd have been well over the limit. It was a mark of how quickly our relationship got serious that we talked about the age issue very early. We agreed that it was a big difference, but we decided not to try to reach final decisions now but just to continue to explore what we had. We found that in spite of our age gap, we had amazingly similar interests, outlooks and tastes. We kept looking for problems, but they didn't arise.

Through the spring, these two issues loomed up above us, while we continued to grow closer and closer. We spent a weekend together in a rented house at Sea Ranch, an utterly beautiful stretch of seacoast three hours north of San Francisco. From our bedroom, high above a field full of wild irises, we looked out across the meadows that rolled down to the edge of the land where the surf slammed up against the cliff. With the windows open, we could hear the waves and the whistles of the hawks overhead. We lay there, taking turns imagining what our future might be.

We didn't say it, except indirectly, but it was clear that we wanted to spend our lives together—a fact that came as a surprise to both of us. The collapse of her marriage plans less than two years earlier had brought her to the point of deciding that she was going to go through the rest of her life as a single person. That was ironic, because on my drive through the narrow lanes of Wales, I had spent hours coming to terms with my own aloneness, and even feeling some relief in realizing that I would no longer have to negotiate everything with someone else.

We went out to dinner that night at a cliff-top restaurant just north of Sea Ranch that looked out over a deep cove. While we waited for our table, we sat in lawn chairs at the edge of the cliff, speaking only occasionally and watching the sun set behind the fog that was piled up along the horizon. Something had happened. We had crossed, unawares, the boundary between possibility and certainty. And that night, as we lay in bed listening to the thump and whish of the waves, we both knew that although we wouldn't take any actions based on our decision until the year was up (the ground rule was undergoing modification), *we were going to be together for good.*

•   •   •

There are no signposts in the sea.

Vita Sackville-West

The next night, I woke up after midnight. Even before I was fully awake, I knew that I was worrying again over whether it was wise to do what I had already in my heart decided to do. How could something that seemed to break all the rules feel so right? I had been raised to think things through, to weigh all the evidence, and not to be hasty. I had spent my whole life being careful and rational. I had been brought up not ever to do anything that I couldn't justify by good sense. I had spent my whole life putting together arguments to justify my behavior, as though living were some extension of a debating competition. I had been raised to make *decisions*, but now I had come to a point in my life where I needed to make a *choice*.

Decisions are made on the basis of evidence and logic, but choices are always an act of will.[5] Many important activities go better on the basis of decisions, but living itself is made up of choices. Decisions start with outside data, on the basis of which the decider tries to evaluate the pluses and minuses and come up with a plan of action. Decisions can be made by anyone, and everyone (using the same inputs and logic) will come up with the similar conclusions. But choices are unique and idiosyncratic. That makes them human. They start with (and express) who we are. Decisions have many possible forms, but choices have only two: *yes* and *no*.

After making a decision, you have to stir up the fires of motivation to get yourself to act on what you have decided. But with a choice, the act of choosing starts the ball of action rolling. Decisions leave you out on the periphery. ("Who decided this?" yells the boss and somebody on the edge of the group looks guilty.) Choices put you (the chooser) in the center of the picture; they are self-motivating, and they lead naturally to commitment.

It had been a choice to leave teaching and enter the community back in 1974. It had been a choice to stay with Mondi during the painful disclosure of her infidelity. And it was a choice, now, to commit myself to Susan. With decisions, you can assess how much of a risk you are taking. With choices, you can't weigh the odds. There aren't odds because you can't flip the coin a hundred times to calculate them. There is just the one life, so there is just the one toss. There isn't even a second try. You can't talk about a right path to take, because *right* means *right* vs. *wrong*, and that is two, and you don't get to retrace your steps and try the other one to see whether it is better. When you choose, there is just whatever path you *do* take and the life that that choice creates for you.

I had learned to make careful decisions from my mother. Now, living a life based on choices felt just as dangerous as she used to make me feel that it was. Loving her two sons, she passed on to us the lesson her life had taught her: that *you couldn't be too careful*. I believed her for more than sixty years. I lived my life carefully, avoiding risk whenever I could. But now, here I was at the end of my programming, walking down a path that wasn't even on her map.

As I came to realize this, I grew calmer. Not that my recognition made the issue less serious—just that I wasn't dumb or thoughtless or irresponsible for not being able to figure it all out in advance. All right, I thought, I'll live from choice. To do that is to live *riskily*.

I imagined standing at the very edge of a tall cliff, leaning forward with my arms out wide, feeling the updraft of wind lifting me up like a ski jumper. . . then leaning and slowly falling into the windrush, until my feet floated up off the earth and I slid forward into the sky and out toward the horizon. I felt a surge of freedom. I was living my life from the heart. It was my choice. It was my life.

•   •   •

I began to have an idea of my life, not as the slow shaping of achievement to fit my preconceived purposes, but as the gradual discovery and growth of a purpose which I did not know.

Johanna Field

We decided to get married the next winter, and as we started planning the event we were once again back in the world of decisions: where to hold the event, whom to invite, what kind of music to have, what kind of food to serve. It was strange. Those next months were full of great busyness, but they felt relatively uneventful. The months before we had made our choice had been outwardly quite ordinary; but they felt enormously eventful. It isn't the events that make a period of your life transitional. It is the deeper inner shifts that take place, the inner turnings that you may not even recognize until you can look back and see that at that point your footsteps curved off in a new direction.

The neutral zone is, as they say in children's stories, where you find *the treasure*. But you can't go out prospecting for it, any more than you can decide to make an ending and put your old life behind you. Life makes those decisions. And *finding* the treasure isn't quite the right verb, for you don't come across what you are seeking, like a statue hidden in the greenery of a garden. It is more like a piece of music that you hear, at first only a few distant notes, but then enough to pick up the tune.

Or perhaps you are the artist. In that case, the new life that you are creating is not put together or chiseled from a block of stone, piece by piece. It is more like a piece of music that you are making up as you go along. Living creatively in the neutral zone involves improvising, finding the way by trial and error. But "making up" a piece of music is too active a metaphor, because in the neutral zone there is often little to do except to wait watchfully as the closer edge of your new life begins to come into focus, rising up out of the depths beyond your sight like something large and strange, floating up to the surface of a pond.

•   •   •

The true use of the imagination is to decipher the present under its teeming incoherency and the anomalies of language. . . As for the Future, your task is not to foresee, but to enable it. All true creation is not a pre-judgment of the Future,. . . . but the apprehending of a new aspect of the present, which is a heap of raw materials bequeathed by the past. . . . Therefore let the future unfurl itself at leisure, like a tree putting forth its branches one by one. From one present moment to another the tree will grow, and when its days are numbered, cease to live. Feel no qualms.

Antoine de Saint-Exupéry

My journey through the neutral zone was like my previous visits to that place, though so much was at stake this time that I kept being tempted to fall back on advice. Yet each time I started to do so, I realized that doing so was the *Way-To* Path that I was trying to avoid. To an extent that I never dared to before, I went where my life led me. I viewed everything I encountered as if it had been prepared for me as part of the new course in which I was currently enrolled: "Finding Your New Life."

I followed *my own way*, not in the sense of the old Sinatra ballad, which is about *my* way as opposed to *everyone else's* way. I followed my own way in the sense of accepting whatever lay along the path that I was following, in the sense of looking at everything as something potentially meaningful, in the sense of imagining that whatever was going on was a message left especially for me. And I followed my way rather than figuring out or planning what I ought to do.

Coming out of this neutral zone, I have done the same thing regarding my work. My choice there was this book, and that represents a scary turn away from the focus on organizations that has made me successful. A voice in the back of my head is sputtering, "What? You're going to walk away from the corporations, that'll pay you five times as much as working with individuals ever will? And what do you base that on? Some passing interest, probably." No, I reply. It's the future, *my* future, and I've just glimpsed it.

For I had discovered that the future is part of the present, like one of those children's puzzles in which strange objects are hidden in the everyday details of the drawing: A swan is cruising up the living room curtains, an airplane dives into a woman's wide hat, and George Washington's head is right there in the rose bush outside the window. The main thing to do is not to hurry up and figure things out, but just to center yourself and wait watchfully.

We don't really have that tradition in our culture—nor do we have an appreciation of the importance of the neutral zone—but here is a description of the state that I found most useful when I came across it in the midst of my own neutral zone. The writer is a German who spent a lifetime studying Japanese spiritual traditions, and in this passage he is describing the Japanese tendency to use a quiet time (or time-out) to focus oneself before tackling a new or a difficult situation:

They do not go there in order to 'meditate' on their own problems, but to surrender themselves to the source of life, whose fluidity relieves a problem of its complexity and allows [one] to exercise his own powers in perfect liberty.[6]

That's the spirituality we gain access to in the neutral zone: the source of life, which is also the creative aspect of the neutral zone.

•   •   •

Living is a form of not being sure, not knowing what's next
or how. The moment you know, you begin to die a little.

Agnes de Mille

As I look back on the neutral zone experience that I have just described, I think: "O.K. That one turned out wonderfully, but you couldn't do that again if you tried. You don't even know what you did, for God's sake!" I'm embarrassed to say that if my present life were to fall apart, I suspect that I'd be right back to trying to figure out what to do (How To. . . How To. . .) to start over again. I am *such a slow learner!* When I am ninety, I'll still be discovering, as if for the first time, that the way of transition simply involves following your path, letting go when it is time, being open to the neutral zone when that is what you need to do, and embracing the new form when it emerges from the shadows at the edge of the present.

ten

Transition and Elderhood

Never have I enjoyed youth so thoroughly as I have in my old age. . . Nothing is inherently and invincibly young except spirit. And spirit can enter a human being perhaps better in the quiet of old age and dwell there more undisturbed than in the turmoil of adventure.

George Santayana

When I was nine, my father bought me a copy of the annual *World Almanac*. The book was a compendium of information and knowledge that ran, then, to about eight-hundred pages and covered almost every topic that someone writing a grade-school report might need to know about. It didn't, of course, tell me the things that I really wanted to know, like What It's All About, Who I'd Be Someday, and How to Be Liked. But its lists of Tallest Mountains (by Continent), Useful Inventions (Dates and Inventors), Cities Over One Million—there were a lot fewer then—Major League Batting Champions, and Life Expectancy (by Sex and Age) were wonderfully reassuring to an inquisitive young boy who wanted to understand the world.

Something that I read the other day made me recall those Life Expectancy tables. I still remember that it said that a male of my age

179

group could expect to live to be sixty-three. That seemed about right to me because my Uncle Billy, the great-uncle for whom I had been named, had just died a year earlier at sixty-three. Although I knew that some people lived longer, and although I had a vague sense of "averages," I got it in my head that men had some kind of internal clock-setting that went off at sixty-three. When you're nine, sixty-three is as far away as another galaxy, so I accepted the news impersonally, like the length of the Amazon and the largest fish ever caught with rod and reel.

There were many reasons why falling in love with Susan when I was sixty-three surprised me, but not the least of them was that at some level of memory and expectation, I had been pretty sure that I'd be dead by that time. Just as Everest was the tallest mountain and Ted Williams batted .406 in 1941, so men died at sixty-three. The *World Almanac* said so.

Except for my father, of course. He died at *fifty*-three, in what the papers called a "boating accident." That made it sound a little more glamorous than it was, for what actually happened was that he took an old dinghy that was so decrepit that it was going to be converted into a planter box for petunias and tried to stand up in it in the middle of Maine's Passamaquoddy Bay, where tidal currents rip along fast enough in some places to create white-water rapids. As though that weren't dangerous enough, he was dead drunk at the time. He fell out. Maine ocean water is very cold and his arthritis limited his mobility, so he probably died fairly quickly. His body was never recovered. He left no note, but since he was very depressed at the time and since he had told my aunt that he "might not come back" from this visit to northern Maine unless he succeeded in getting his drinking under control, I always regarded his death as a suicide.

So I have had my own reasons for viewing the years after fifty as problematic, but I am not alone in that view. People have frequently noted that our society is a thankless one in which to grow old. Our elderly are not respected, as they are in more traditional cultures, because we have had a youth-oriented culture for a couple of centuries, That fact actually makes a kind of social sense, although it is usually

treated as though it were part of a misguided and inexplicable con-
spiracy against old people. The huge and rapid scientific and technical developments (which, ironically, have extended the average
lifetime fifteen years since I was nine) meant that it is the younger,
more recently educated people who understand what's happening
today. In that practical sense, they are more valuable to society than
the older people are, and societies have a way of favoring their valuable assets.

In a society where the most important knowledge is the unchang-
ing lore of special geographical locations, typical patterns of animal
behavior, the ripening times of food-plants and botanical remedies,
and the signs of changes in the weather, old people are priceless
storehouses of knowledge. That kind of knowledge isn't something
that you pick up in quickly. It is only in seeing those things happen
again and again through the years that you can sift out all the irrele-
vancies and identify the core of critical knowledge.

In addition to this lore, living for a long time gives you another
kind of knowledge that was also very important in traditional societies. Because they had grown up and grown old in a society that recognized and celebrated the phases of the year and the stages of a
lifetime, the elder members of such societies had gone through rituals that reenacted the three-phase pattern of ending, neutral zone,
and beginning over again many times. At the ceremonies held at the
seasonal turning points of the year, or at the death of one ruler and
the accession of another, their attention had been repeatedly drawn
to those three transitional stages.

Our own elderly people not only lack the practical, socially useful
knowledge that yesterday's elders had. They also lack the familiarity
with and understanding of transition that those elders had because
they have grown old without consciously going through meaningful
transitions. Their lives have been full of change, of course. But our
society has not prepared them to let go of an old life and to grow a
new one. That, too, makes a kind of sense, because in practical terms
the mechanistic idea of change has had greater utilitarian value than
the more organic concept of transition has.

The focus on change has given us the power to remake the world, but it has also meant that our society has not developed comparably effective ways of dealing with the human dimensions of change. Our society has thereby shortchanged both the elderly and itself, since every society needs to have recognized ways (with living exemplars) of how to renew itself at the individual level. We need models of how to replenish our lives periodically, so they do not just run down and peter out, as the lives of so many of our old people do. Having overlooked transition as our society has, it isn't surprising that we lack elders to serve as guides and advisers at life's turning points.

Most of today's efforts to reaffirm the societal and personal value of age and aging are simply spitting into the wind, for these efforts do not build on any ground where the old have a real advantage over the young. To establish the value to the society of its elders, they must be shown to possess something that the society needs. Here is where transition represents something that has both personal and societal values, for it is the dynamic by which people develop and gain access to the world of the sacred. If people can recognize that as they age, they will not only find their own lives more meaningful, but will also become the resource to younger people that they are not now.

●   ●   ●

To understand things we must have been once in them and then have come out of them; so that first there must be captivity and then deliverance, illusion followed by disillusion, enthusiasm by disappointment. He who is still under the spell and he who has never felt the spell are equally incompetent.

Amiel

Taking our cue from the machinery and the data that dominate our world, we usually view knowledge as something that accumulates piecemeal over time. You start out with a little, and then you gradually pick up more and more. It's like possessions: they pile up over time. But passive accumulation isn't the way that you learn the most important things that you know about the world. The way you do that is much more the way that Amiel describes in the quotation above. First you are immersed in the knowledge, then you get distance from it (and even deny it), and then you return to a new relation with it.

That is the kind of knowledge that the experience of transition leads to. First you know, and then you let go of what you knew—or thought that you knew, because the disenchantment process makes the old "reality" seem very unreal. Then, during the neutral zone phase of transition, you no longer experience the old reality and may feel that you lack a reality now or that your reality is confused or crazy. But that state also passes, and you return to your life again. Yet it isn't the same life—it's a new, transformed life. It's you-but-not-the-old-you. Like the Technicolor Kansas that Dorothy returned to, which had been black-and-white when she left it.

The only way you acquire this kind of knowledge—which is called "wisdom" to distinguish it from that which is acquired in the ordinary way—is to have gone through a profound life-transition, or rather to go through a number of them in the process of aging. Only after you have done that do you see the old world with new eyes and understand it in depth. Arthur Schopenhauer was speaking tongue in cheek, though truthfully, when he said that a person "who sees two or three generations is like one who sits in the conjurer's booth at the fair and sees the tricks two or three times. They are meant to be seen only once."[1] The single-view reality is what a number of spiritual traditions have called the world of illusion, although its simplicity makes it an appropriate view for young children.

Our society is not very sensitive to the knowledge that comes from seeing the tricks over and over again, for it is created over time by a dynamic and maturing relation between the knower and the known, rather than being just *there* to be acquired as rationalistic knowledge is. Do we discount such knowledge because we fail to appreciate the importance of the transition process, or do we fail to understand the transition process because we have forgotten the importance of such knowledge? I don't know. But I do know that the two difficulties go together.

I know that we avoid endings whenever possible, and we steer clear whenever we can of the neutral-zone emptiness. Endings feel like failure to us, and at a deeper level they awaken in us the fear of death. So we use the busyness and structure and status of work and family life to hide ending it from view. Only when life makes death an unavoidable fact do most of us overcome this aversion, but by then the resonance of that grand event is so great that the little-deaths of endings are often drowned out in the mighty music of the final scene.

All those transition points in a traditional person's lifetime were treated as practice sessions for the ultimate ending that they would finally encounter. Death is a shocking, new experience in our society. It is no wonder that we use what I earlier called "the additive fallacy" to avoid endings, believing in doing so that if we just keep adding and adding to what we have, we'll end up with something new and will avoid the need to make any endings.

But it is not just endings that we fear. The aloneness and emptiness that are often felt in the neutral zone are just about as fearful for many modern people as endings are, for they reawaken in us all our childhood fears of abandonment. And since most modern people no longer know the natural world well, the idea that we need a fallow time or a time of gestation isn't natural to us any longer. Whenever we can't see that anything is happening—and you usually can't in the neutral zone—we doubt that anything can "really" be going on. And the chaos, that state of pure energy that is experienced either as a jumble or as a time of empty nothingness, makes us feel out of control and a little crazy.

We fail to see that real new beginnings, the kind that revitalize and inaugurate a new order of things, come out of that chaotic neutral zone. Instead, we try to make a fresh start by an act of will, putting together a plan that lays out a whole sequence of actions that we will take to transform ourselves or our worlds. When the plans don't work as we expect them to, we shake our heads sadly and conclude that either the plans themselves were defective or there was a problem with how the plans were implemented. The idea that we failed because we tried to make a *change* do the work of a *transition* doesn't occur to us.

It is not just individuals that do this. Corporations and government agencies reorganize, merge, and undertake culture-changes, and then wonder why people can't get through the transitional turmoil that ensues. They pay consultants to help them to "envision" a new future for themselves, and then announce Big Changes as though all people had to do to get through them successfully was to understand what the outcome was going to be and why it was necessary. Most organizations have no idea that real renewal requires a conscious ending of how things used to be.[2] Think how much more praise and reward people get for making even the most dubious new beginnings in the organizational world than they get for making absolutely essential endings.

Although people talk a lot about how difficult change is, it is really transition that is difficult. It is, in fact, common for both organizations and individuals to use change to avoid the transitions that would truly transform their existence.

- Individuals walk out of a relationship, rather than letting go of the *approach* to relationships that made them unsuccessful and unsatisfying in the past—and will continue to do so in the future.
- Organizations find that some particular change (that they made without any attention to the transitions it caused) did not work. But rather than giving up on that make-the-change-and-forget-the-transition approach, they repeat it by initiating another change—and are amazed when that change doesn't work either.
- Individuals look for a new job rather than facing the attitudes and behaviors toward work and toward authority-figures that made them unsuccessful in all of their past jobs. They don't ask what it is time for them to let go of. Instead

they say they need to start over—so they make a change.

- Organizations try to copy a competitor's successful product, and then try again with another when the first one isn't a winner. They do not let go of their strategy of imitating the competition, and doing something original instead—even though originality is exactly what gave the competition its advantage.

- Individuals decide to move to a new house or a new town, rather than letting go inwardly of the old way of living that lacked meaning. They make a change rather than making the more profound transition, which would put them on a genuinely new life-path.

In the modern world, very few individuals or organizations understand the need to relinquish periodically all that they have depended upon for their meaning and security and to explore the neutral zone in depth, in order to discover there the thread leading to a new life.

And here it is that the old clearly do have an advantage over the young—or would, if they too weren't often so ignorant of the way of transition. I think, though, that I am stating the case too harshly. For what the old lack is an *affirmation* of the wisdom that many of them, in fact, do possess from living through a lifetime of transitions. So we have a secret cadre-in-waiting, a group of people whose experience has taught them, individually, what once whole generations were taught by their wise ones. To recognize this wisdom will benefit both its carriers and the society at large.

•   •   •

Age puzzles me. I thought it was a quiet
time. . . I grow more intense as I age.

Florida Scott-Maxwell

As I have thought back over my own life in the process of writing this book, I am struck by how young I was when I started trying to create a career and a family: in my mid-twenties when I came out of the army, I started working, and then I got married. It wasn't so much that I was young in years or experience or that I was unsophisticated, as that I was *undeveloped*. I knew so little about myself or about other people. More precisely, I'd say that I knew nothing about how others look when you have seen into your own heart. I was glib and full of ideas back then. Being older than Mondi (she was only nineteen and I was twenty-six when we married), I found it easy to think of myself as more mature. But maturity was years and years down the path ahead of me.

In the twenty-five years after I started a family and a career, I was much less interested in maturing than I was in *growing*. Those were the sixties and seventies, and I was active in the Human Potential Movement. We all talked a lot about growth. We went to *growth* centers like Esalen Institute and we attended encounter and Gestalt groups, where everyone was self-consciously trying to *grow*. In one sense, that was just California at that particular time, but Americans in general have always admired growth. We admire the fastest growing companies and the cities that grew the most in the past decade. Magazines list the national economies that are growing the fastest, ranking them in descending order of growth speed. Bigger is better and bigger-faster is better still. Even the doubters become believers when the growth in question involves their own assets.

There is another kind of growth, which is much harder to measure. Fewer people admire it or seek it out today. It doesn't involve expansion, simply the mysterious process of maturing. Its goal is not an increase in size (or intelligence or sophistication or experience or skill), but simply *ripening*. This is not growth by acquisition, but growth by development or evolution. We cross the barriers to this kind of growth not by breaching or surmounting them, the way we do when we are bent on growth as increase. We overcome the barriers to growth as development when we are able to view our problems as signals that it is time to let go of the way in which we have been seeing and doing things and initiate a developmental transition.

The barriers to this kind of growth are overcome whenever we stop viewing our flaws and problems as things to be solved or removed, and start viewing them as signals. What the problems are, really, are old solutions that have outlived their usefulness. From that point of view, whenever we do away with a problem instead of listening to its message, we trigger a string of events that lands us in trouble.

Remember the story of *Sleeping Beauty*? The curse that put that young woman to sleep was invoked by a "wicked" spirit that wanted to hurt her because the spirit had been left off the invitation list to her parents' wedding. On a literal level the exclusion is understandable ("Who needs troublemakers at a wedding?"), but what the story is saying at its deeper levels is that attempting to exclude the bad and increasing the good simply increases the destructive power of whatever is excluded.

You encounter the phenomenon whenever you try to banish from your mind a bad (frightening, immoral or embarrassing) thought. Such an action simply increases its power and interrupts the natural flow of thoughts and feelings, in which they follow one another in fluid succession without any of them becoming overwhelming. In the metaphorical language of *Sleeping Beauty*, once people lose their healthy connection with that flow and the access it gives them to the wellsprings of their lives, they "go to sleep." That is, they enter a suspended state in which they stop developing.

A similar point is made by the biblical story of Jacob and Esau, although this time the metaphor is not excluding someone from an event but excluding a son from his rightful place as the head of the family. Jacob takes the birthright away from his brother, who is described in metaphors associated in folk wisdom with danger and evil: he is darker, hairier, not so civilized as Jacob. Paradoxically, this wrongful action gives Esau so much power over Jacob that years later when they meet, Jacob is terrified of his brother and projects hostile and violent intents upon him. He prays to God, "Deliver me, I pray thee, from the hand of my brother, from the hand of Esau, for I fear him, lest he come and slay us all, the mothers and the children."[3]

Amazingly—at least from the viewpoint of common sense—the unfairly excluded sibling is not even bitter, but comes seeking a reconciliation. The story illustrates the point that the poet, Rilke, made in his letter to a young writer: "Perhaps everything that frightens us is, in its deepest essence, something helpless that wants our love."[4] The problem, the flaw, the inferior element is not only *not bad*, but is the very thing that has the power to rescue the person who, without it, is not whole and cannot develop and mature. It is, to continue referring to the world of folk and wisdom stories, the archetypal story of the inconspicuous and overlooked youngest child, who turns out to be the one who wins in the end or who saves the day.

Such victory always enters by the back door, not only being achieved by the underdog, but also by means of methods that appear to be unpromising, or even that look at first like a mistake. Little Dorothy, the youngest character in *The Wizard of Oz*, saves her relatives' dried up farmland and ramshackle farmhouse by going on a wondrous journey, that she would never have taken if she had succeeded in reaching the safety of the cyclone cellar. If she hadn't failed in her attempt to escape the storm, there'd have been no story and no salvation—just a ruined, old house. Later, she returns from her transformative journey with the new power it gave her only because she *doesn't* succeed in getting aboard the Wizard's departing hot air balloon. Had she not failed to make it into the balloon's basket, she would never have come back with the power to change things—just with some pretty new shoes.

*   *   *

We neither get better or worse as we
get older, but more like ourselves.

Robert Anthony

Every culture has its own favored image of movement through space. Ours is the straight line, the shortest distance from A to B. Getting closer to B—"getting there," wherever *there* is—is what we like to call "making progress." Further is better—further ahead, further up, further down, further in, further out. Far out, we say. Far out! The typical journey of American history has been a one-way trip: from the Old World to the New World, from the seaboard colonies to the western frontier, or from the farm to the city. Americans have always been looking for something that is out or over "there"—or else fleeing from something that is "here." Either way it's been a one-way trip to some destination where things will be better, where you can escape from your past and start over again. American lives often have a two-dimensional quality, like the maps on which their travels can be traced.

But other cultures, including most of those that have produced the spiritual treasures of humankind, have seen movement differently. Not from here to there, but here to there and back again. The natural figure is circular. As the *Tao Te Ching* says, "Going on means going far,/Going far means returning."[5] The great journeys are pilgrimages to a sacred place, and then after the journey has done its transformative work, pilgrimages return back home again. No matter how enormous the discoveries are, they are meant to be brought home into everyday life. As the Zen saying puts it, "After enlightenment, the laundry." Although, of course, it's not the same laundry any more.

When we look back on our lives, we can see either the linear or the circular journey, depending on which we are looking for. Americans usually opt for the linear. When they do, they find a stretch of time that can be segmented into periods or stages. That is how I was asking you to view your own life back in Chapter Two, when I urged you to divide your life into chapters. Each chapter would have told a piece of the story, A to B, B to C, C to D, and they would have been lined up one, two, three.

In some of the parts of this book, I have followed that pattern myself, with linear segments from (or one-way trips through) some aspect of my own life. Keeping things in chronological order that way shows you a lot, especially about cause and effect, and I think that it was a useful way to view my career and my marriage. But the linearity of A to B is all entropy, time ticking away, oneself getting older.

When I look back over those same two periods, I can just as readily see another figure: great looping round-trips, quest-and-homecoming journeys like Dorothy's jaunt to the Land of Oz and back. You can talk about transition in either context. In the linear context, it's the segue between one life-segment and the next, as well as being the process that disengages us from the first phase, turns us around, and plugs us into the second phase. In the circular-journey context, transition is an analytical way of talking about the journey itself.

Through the journey-lens, I can see the story of my marriage to Mondi beginning when I set off on a quest, following a yellow brick road called Being Married. I was something of a tin woodsman, a man without much feeling, and Mondi was my Wizard. I had never been seriously in love before, and I believed that Mondi was magic. She would tell me or show me how to find the hidden door to my heart. She was going to transform me.

But as with Dorothy, my quest turned out to be a complicated one, not a simple trip where you take care of business on the first try and head home for supper. As I look back on it now, forty years later, it looks to me as though I had to go on at least four of these miniquests during my years with Mondi. The first time I was searching for the person who would rescue me from my loneliness. She liked to say that I had been alone, drinking at a bar, when she first saw me in a social setting, and that such isolation was my natural habitat. In the beginning that was true, though with and through her, I came out of my empty private world and found what it was to be connected intimately with someone else. We lived out the first phase of our marriage that way, but as with Dorothy, one trek was not enough to finish the job.

Then, through her dissatisfactions with our lack of communication, she presented me with a "problem," and I started struggling to get to know myself and to understand the world of feeling. Again, she was my wizard. She had the answers. This was a very rocky journey. I kept thinking that I had reached the desired end, only to find that I needed to perform yet another "task." Years later, when she discovered the lump in her breast, I was still trying to identify and perform the tasks that she set for me.

If this were told as a linear story, I could divide those years from the mid-sixties to the late-eighties into two or three segments, corresponding to my work-history or my writing or where I lived or the doings of my family. But if I were to tell them as a journey, those years were all part of the same cycle—the cycle which was devoted to learning about feelings. That cycle played itself out into another drought, which came to an end with the affair with her therapist.

That storm almost blew me off the face of the earth, and for a time I thought that I had nothing more to learn from her. I didn't admire her any longer—I didn't even like her much of the time. But slowly I learned something from her that she didn't even know she was teaching. As I saw the pain and hunger and weakness that had made her vulnerable to his seduction, I started seeing her with compassion. I had often heard about compassion and read about it, but I am embarrassed to say that I had really never before felt it for anyone. I had often been sympathetic or concerned for someone else, but I had never accepted someone absolutely as they were and loved them even for the weaknesses that I wished that they had not had.

I lost a lot of things when I did that. An invisible Toto had tipped over her screen and had revealed her in all her imperfection. There she was, caught in the act of betrayal. There were many months during that time when all I could do was to hold on. The best I could manage was to stand my ground as the wronged husband. But she didn't let me off the hook so easily as that. She had the gall to protect her last shreds of vulnerability by saying that she would not even talk to me about my grief and hurt! Betrayal upon betrayal! She had wounded me deeply, and now she wouldn't even talk about it. (I have to admit with some embarrassment that I was actually trying to use her earlier lessons against her, for I wanted to talk about "my feelings.") Turning down that request showed that she was a hypocrite, I thought.

I couldn't see at that time—it was simply too great a reach for me—what a gift her refusal was. For if she had melted and acknowledged that she had hurt me, and if she had said that she felt awful about that, I could have set myself up as "forgiving." Her worthiness-tally would have fallen many points and mine would have risen commensurably. I would have become more comfortable, but I would also have lost my opportunity to mature, to ripen. For it was only in the slow process of understanding and accepting her—with all her double standards and lack of empathy—that I learned to feel compassionately toward her. She gave me the chance for that experience, even though it nearly destroyed both of us. Once again she was my teacher—in the sense of someone who causes you to learn, not someone who instructs you consciously.

Told as a circular journey, the story of my marriage would have to be the story of an education. Mondi was the most important teacher I ever had, not because she was right about me—although she always claimed to be and often actually was—but because being around her made me learn. She was more like the "challenge" in Toynbee's story of the rise of civilization in the Nile Valley, a challenge that pushed me to the point where I either had to hold on and sink with the ending of my old life or let go and follow the new trajectory of my own development.

But that third journey into discovery wasn't my last. She had one last lesson for me, and she hadn't intended to teach that one either. All she was doing was dying. But with her lifelong hunger for life's experiences, she was embracing death as an old friend. Several times during her final months, she shared things with me that she had never told me before about her abusive childhood. She told me about her only way of escaping the hopelessness and misery that she felt during those early years. Back then, she would sometimes come to the point where she thought that she could not, even for just a few minutes longer, stand the pain that her parents' cruelty was causing her. But then, as a gift from heaven, would come a thought: "I can kill myself; death will save me."

To an extent that I hardly suspected until it was near at hand, death had always been her friend. When we were on vacation on the island in the Great Barrier Reef, just a month before she died, we were resting together in our cottage, looking out across a lawn where big monitor lizards bellied through the grass. Beyond the palm trees and across a little white strip of beach and out to sea, a storm was piling up dark clouds. I asked her if she knew Emily Dickinson's poem that begins,

Because I could not stop for Death—
He kindly stopped for me—
The Carriage held but just Ourselves—
And Immortality.

"No," she replied. "But I like it already. Say it the rest of it to me."

I couldn't remember the rest of it, but I promised to look it up and give it to her when we got home.

When we finally did get home, however, she was having such a hard time that I never got around to doing that. I was too busy keeping things going and watching her live right up to the final beat of her heart, before she turned and vanished into the darkness.

Watching her die was not a gift that drew me to her so much as it drew me to myself. If she had died at some point early in our marriage, I wouldn't have thought that I could go on, because so much of my well-being was tied up in the wizard-things that I still hoped that she could do for me. If she had died only a couple of years before she did, we would have left so many things unresolved and I would have been so full of turmoil that I couldn't have gained from her the gifts she ultimately bestowed on me.

Whatever it was that originally attracted you to a relationship—or a job or a neighborhood or a lifestyle—isn't the actual benefit that the thing turns out to hold for you. And whatever it is that keeps you engaged in an undertaking is often similarly beside the point. Those apparent benefits are just the window dressing, the bargain specials (which don't, it turns out, come in our size—thank goodness). The actual lesson or payoff or effect is discovered only over time and often from a quite unexpected quarter. It was Mondi's great charisma that attracted me and, for a long time, held me to her. In logical terms, perhaps we should have split up years earlier when our fundamental differences began to cause us great pain. But if I had parted from her then, I would have missed so much. For at the very end, burning up in the hot fire of her own mortality, she gave me back myself.

Seeing my marriage as the kind of long, punctuated quest that ended up bringing me back home to myself is a very different way of seeing life and transition. In this view, the story of a life is not a chronicle, punctuated by dates and places and incidents. It is more like a myth, a story with the classic pattern of challenge and response. In that latter view, the story of my marriage is a deep tale of withdrawal and return. I left the world of aloneness, stepped across some threshold of transformation into the land of relationship, and then finally back out again. But the solitary world I reentered at her death was as alive, complex and full of meaning as the Kansas that Dorothy returned to. Further, it was *my* world.

Coming into my own world was, I think, the significance of that dream that I described early in this book, where I waited for Mondi in our car and then finally gave up and drove home alone. I was deeply troubled in the dream by the thought that perhaps I should have stayed and waited for her, or that I ought to have gone back and tried to find her. As I reread that dream now, the final line in my notebook strikes me afresh: "I waited for her, sitting on the passenger side of the car for a few minutes. When she didn't come back, I moved over into the driver's seat and started the car."

As I said, she gave me back to myself.

•   •   •

[It is gravity that] causes water to flow, draws it away from its spherical form and makes it follow a more or less linear and determined course. Yet water continually strives to return to its spherical form. It finds many ways of maintaining a rhythmical balance between the spherical form natural to it and the pull of earthly gravity. . . . What causes water to follow such a winding course [as a meander]? Its endeavor to complete the circle is here only partially successful, as it cannot flow back uphill to its starting point. Right at the beginning of its circulatory movement it is drawn downhill and in following this downward pull it swings alternatively from side to side.

Theodor Schwenk

You can see any period of your life as the journey of withdrawal and return, and whenever you do, new meanings will be revealed to you. They are the kinds of meanings that, taken as a whole, represent your particular curriculum of training to be an elder. If you experience your whole life as made up of such circular journeys, your past stretches back behind one like those big, looping, meandering rivers that you see when fly over the American midwest. Everyone's life looks like that, in retrospect, though many people are apologetic at what an apparently random and wandering course or pathway they have followed. Rather than viewing such lives as evidence of chance or confusion, however, we ought to recognize that they are as natural to the flow of a life as the curving watercourse way is natural to the river.

The *meander* is the technical name for the loop in the course of a river, and it was named for a river in Greece whose bed followed such a path. The meander that sends the living water out away from the fall line and then back again, is life's natural path, I think. Straightened out, canalized, Department-of-Engineers pathways are as artificial in life as they are in riverbeds. In both cases they are overrationalized and ultimately dangerous because they do not provide a way for the living current to pass through without eroding the land or flooding it. They are like those efforts at self-improvement and personal virtue that are based on excluding the dark side of life. They are like the chemical fertilizers that provide all the right artificial nutriments, but give the soil no organic matter to restore its texture.

The idea that development ought to include all the dark and curvy uniqueness of a person isn't some weird, New Age view of life. When Jesus told his disciples, almost two thousand years ago, "You, therefore, must be perfect, as your heavenly Father is perfect,"[6] he was not telling them that they had to be utterly without blemish like the hood of a new car. The Greek adjective that is translated as "perfect" was *teleios,* which means "having reached the appropriate or appointed *telos* ('end' in the sense of 'goal' or 'purpose')."[7] He is saying that we are meant to be whole, fully formed, fully developed. The end of development is to become the unique individuals that we essentially are. It is what Jung spoke of as the process of *individuation*. To be "without sin," in this sense, is very close to what is meant by the words, "mature" or "ripe."

This is where older people can become *elders*. If they can perceive, understand, and appreciate the meaning of the meandering path they have followed, they can play such a significant social role by helping younger people to understand the significance of the transitions in their own lives. They can help others to discover the deeper meaning (or the developmental significance) of otherwise negative life events. For they have encountered the problems that signal a time of transition often enough to recognize them and take them seriously. They can appreciate, in this context, the importance of failure, for they can see that it is through our failures (where we lose the life that we hoped to gain) that we enter into the developmental transitions that help us to grow beyond the superficial, glib, brittle self-confidence of youth.

The elderly have taken the trip often enough to recognize the turns in the road. They can appreciate the tremendous value of living through times when letting go is the only appropriate response to life. Important though perseverance is, they know how easily it can turn into a refusal to get the message that life is trying to deliver. For in many cases, being unwilling to accept defeat—though celebrated in the world of sports and warfare—is a guarantee that one will never learn the lessons that must be learned if one is to mature.

That is why the elders that we need so badly in our success-obsessed society are not the natural-born winners who rose to the top without a setback. Such people are easy to idealize, but they have little to teach us. What elders need to help younger people learn is that without releasing the fruits of one season, they cannot blossom into the next. Such elders can show us, because they have done it many times, how to let go of who we have been to clear the ground for the growth of who we are becoming. They can help us to understand the transition-related emotions of grief (sadness for what we have let go of), disorientation (when we are lost in the neutral zone), and fear (when the challenges of the unknown new beginnings are overwhelming).

Old people, if they have learned from the transitions they have been through, grow more tolerant. They see that wholeness is the goal, and that to exclude anything is a brief and shallow victory that leads to ultimate defeat. They can help us to counterbalance our society's overemphasis on worldly success, not by scorning success but by disidentifying from the outcomes of the efforts that they, like anyone else, make. To do one's best and then to let outcomes be what they will is both to acknowledge realistically how often outcomes are beyond our control and to guard against the neurotic attempts at controlling how things turn out—efforts that lead to everything from defensiveness to dishonesty.

It is salutary to note that the word "success" originally had nothing to do with "good" results, much less with the accumulation of wealth or honors. It meant simply *whatever follows after something.* Success was a neutral word, like *outcome,* so the term *ill-success,* that one encounters in Shakespeare and other pre-eighteenth-century writers, is not an oxymoron. The gift of the elderly is a respect for this kind of success (which represents reality, after all) and a mistrust of any focus on the efforts at self-aggrandizement that pass today for living "successfully."

Elders can do these things not because they are nobler or more virtuous than younger people, but because they have the good fortune to live in life's richest phase. That is not to say that they may not have pain and grief, but simply that they can at least see beyond life's window dressing. Their only inevitable sadness is that the living they can at last savor is also running out. But they can see and appreciate the lives they have lived as journeys that they have been on.

The journey metaphor tells us about many important things. It reminds us that every time in life has its baggage and that our attempts to become something often require us to pay a fare. Journeys, like portions of our lifetimes, have their announced destinations, but it is also common to discover that whatever the purported destination, the journey was its own justification.

That journeys carry us along to *their* destination, not ours, helps to make sense out of the experience that we have already noted of finding that you are (or are not) still *on the beam* as you journey along. This experience is so much more important than having a purpose, in the sense of something that can be paraphrased. It is the experience of "homing in" on something, or being tuned in to something, some inner thing.

A journey may take us to Canterbury or to Mecca, but really all journeys are pilgrimages. A journey may be a business trip, but again they all are and *what a business it is that we are engaged in!* And they are all ultimately homecomings—but my, my, hasn't Ithaca changed in our absence! We are always getting away—away from the Czar, away from Egypt, away from an old life. It is always a New World we sail toward.

Wherever the journey starts and whatever its destination may be, the real direction of journeying is toward a deeper realism—deeper or higher: directions get confused as you get closer to the bone. Every disenchantment along the way (thank you, Mondi) is a little awakening, a momentary glimpse behind the veil, a temporary experience of looking through a suddenly transparent world. But the moving on, even though it is only from illusion to illusion, is important too, for only by that movement is one prepared for and brought to that final transition through which one dies to a new life.

Perhaps that is as good a definition of transition to end with as there is: *the natural process by which one dies to a new life.*

eleven

Beginning a New Life

Living is a form of not being sure, not knowing what's next or how. The moment you know how, you begin to die a little.

Agnes de Mille

This book started with an ending and it will finish with a beginning. That is strange, but it is appropriate too, because that is the shape of transition. Inanimate things start and then they stop, but in the dynamic process through which organisms grow and become, endings come first and beginnings come last. That is the shape of the birth-journey through which we left our original nest and entered the world, and it is the shape of the dying that will take us out of the world and into whatever lies beyond it. That is the shape of transformation and renewal, wherever they occur, and it is the shape of the mythic journeys that describe transformation and renewal in metaphorical terms.

In transition, whatever comes next holds sway over what went before it. Transition is a great game of stone-paper-and-scissors, where whatever comes next—whatever *succeeds*, as we were saying before—automatically wins. The new thing carries the day, spring supplants winter, the new year sends the old year packing. But there is no antagonism in this. Just succession. As long as our transitions continue, we are success-ful.

As I sit here, working on my manuscript in our bedroom, I hear Susan running bathwater on the other side of the door. I look back over five years that I could not have imagined in advance. This particular transition, which I started by trying to avoid, has taken me into really new territory. Nothing about my first sixty years prepared me for the present. I can see clearly now that life's segments (me, aged fifty-five to sixty, for example) operate on different rules from those that govern the transitions between the segments (me, aged 60 to 65). That later period, which I am just coming out of, has certainly been a transition.

Writing about the points at which a natural substance goes through a phase transition, James Geick noted:

> As singular boundaries between two realms of existence [e.g., from liquid to gas or from unmagnetized to magnetized], phase transitions tend to be highly nonlinear in their mathematics. The smooth and predictable behavior of matter in any one phase tends to be little help in understanding the transitions.[1]

Amen! That is one reason why being in transition is so confusing. It's not just that the new chapter will work differently. It's also that the transition that gets you to the new chapter is going to follow its own rules too. A lot of the disorientation that we pass off as the result of dealing with something new is really just the product of being in transition.

I think back on my inner debates over the age difference between Susan and me, over my perplexity about how long I ought to wait before I married again, over my anxiety about what my children and my friends would say when I told them that I was getting married again—or, worse, what they *wouldn't* say, but would think. I thought that I was struggling with the future, but I was really struggling with the transition process, *the way that the future entered my life*. But that transition time was amazingly rich, for as I wrestled with all those issues inwardly, I was also making huge choices.

What I was choosing was not only a person to marry, but also a person to become; what I was choosing was not just a new life but a new way of living it. For in the process of choosing to marry Susan, I was discovering that I wanted to live from this point on from the inside out—out of my heart and into the world. This meant that I had to move forward, creating a future for myself, and that the path along which I moved from past to future was a stretch of living that no one had ever crossed before.

Oh, countless people had remarried before, of course. But no one had ever been me, in love with her, before. That didn't mean that we could make dumb decisions—just that the answers weren't printed upside down in small type at the bottom of the page. We'd have to find the "right answers" for ourselves. My ticket was good for one trip only. It was mine. I couldn't use anyone else's.

•   •   •

Time is a dressmaker specializing in alterations.

Faith Baldwin

Living rationally, conceptually, and reasonably had always let me divide things into issues. It had lined things up into cause-and-effect sequences. It had laid out alternatives, under which there were mental lists, pro and con. The results had always been complex patterns of factors and variables, so the decisions certainly weren't easy. But at least I had the data right there in front of me, grouped into categories. It might be risky, but the risks came from how hard it was to weight the different variables and how often big decisions hinged on comparing apples with oranges. The risks were real, but they were calculable. I always had the feeling that I could figure out the right thing to do.

Living from the heart presented me with different and unfamiliar kinds of risk. The issues and the connections dissolved, and the decisions unraveled into shifting, swirling, billowing patterns of shapes. Things no longer lined up into categories, and they kept changing. One day I felt confident, and the next day I was all set to give up. The alternatives were no longer things that I could study; instead they kept morphing into something else, like shadows cast by flickering firelight. The risk was not simply that of making the wrong decision. It was the risk of not being able to bring reality into focus. The risk was not being able to understand what was going on.

I came across a quote the other day from the Indian philosopher, Rabindranath Tagore: "When old words die out on the tongue, new melodies break forth from the heart; and where the old tracks are lost, new country is revealed with its wonders." That was reassuring. You let go of the old way and you take hold of the new way. Simple.

But how was I to know that what I was feeling were *my* new melodies? What if they were simply old melodies from a nearby station, bleeding over onto my wavelength? Then I read Henry Miller's comment that "*Confusion* is a word we have invented for an order which is not yet understood." Great. But how do you understand it when you finally do, and how do you know that your understanding isn't self-deception? And isn't *confusion* ever just a state in and of itself. . . and is it ever a terminal condition?

•   •   •

We are adhering to life now with our last muscle, the heart.

Djuna Barnes

I have come out of the past five years with a great sympathy for people who toss in the towel and try either to retreat back into some old security or to fast-forward through a change (any change!) that will make their lives different. But, having chosen neither of those options, I have also gained a new sense of myself—a sense based much less on my ability to think things through than on the purely subjective experience of being the one to whom my life was happening.

The situation that precipitated this shift simply intensified the natural process of living and aging. Yet, although it is natural, it came as a surprise to me. I had put so much energy into understanding life conceptually and so much faith that such understanding would teach me whatever I needed to know, that I am shocked to realize that I am not in any way wiser for my effort. Wisdom, I discover at this late hour, comes from living itself.

Shifting my attention from understanding to living from the heart brought me another gift as well: I unexpectedly found a wide diversity of my own inner resources opened up before me. In the organizational world where I have been working, *diversity* is the term usually given to the racial, ethnic, gender, or typological mix—the opposite of the old white, male stereotype that corporations used to cultivate. In my own neutral zone, I discovered another kind of diversity, an inner one, a personal one that made me feel like a one-man cast of characters. I found that I was so *diverse,* so full of confusing differences and complexities, that I changed by the minute and at any particular instant hardly recognized myself.

This took some getting used to. To find pleasure in my own subjective mutability meant that I had to be willing to let go of feeling good, whenever that positive feeling began to give way to something darker. It meant that I had to be willing to let good ideas slip away, on the grounds that they'd either turn up again or that something equally good would replace them—or, if that is how it turned out, that I could make it without any good ideas that day. It meant trusting that going flat and feeling dull was as much a prelude to a new time of excitement and interest as it was a finale to the previous time of excitement and interest.

This was all new and strange, however. For I had spent my whole life holding onto good feelings and trying to banish bad ones. I had carried around pocket notebooks to catch good ideas, and had felt irritated when I "lost" them by not recording them. But living in the mutable world of feeling was different. The notebook that I sometimes carried now was less to trap a fleeing idea than to provide a verbal mirror in which to watch my own process. This shift from content to process was something that I couldn't have done before I met up with age, for until then I was trying to hold time at bay.

It is ironic to realize that one of the gifts I have received from get-ting old is the ability to be in the moment. I've been trying to learn to do that for the past thirty-five years, but it has been only with the natural slowing down of my mind and with the losses that I have been through that I am starting to find the present moment suffi-cient to itself. Loss has given me that gift, not by "teaching" me that moments are limited and precious. (That would be learning it the conceptual way.) And the writers I used to read, who urged the same shift in awareness, couldn't "teach" me that either. It is something that came only with time and with the natural sorting process that goes on after loss. As the mud swirls around in the watery pan, the gold-flakes settle of their own weight. Time doesn't fly—it swirls, and the moments settle of from their own gravity. Without serious loss, the water isn't agitated enough to make that happen.

There were other gifts of age that I discovered as my I settled into my new marriage. When I was younger, I treated my own life as though it were one of many that I might live. I don't know whether I used to think that I still had time left to take a second run down the life-course, or whether life was just less indelible to me back then. You might think that recognizing that this was my one-and-only life and that its reality was dyed right into the fiber would have made me more tentative and careful. But in fact, it made me more decisive and willing to risk everything. No more practice sessions; this was the big game itself. No more trying, just go-for-broke.

One night when Susan and I had been dating for four or five months, we went to see *Good Will Hunting*, which had just come out. In the movie the young hero was working with a middle-aged psy-chotherapist whose wife had died. I found myself watching and lis-tening carefully to find out how this other widower had dealt with his loss and what it could teach me about my own. But as the movie went on, an unexpected shift occurred within me, and I found my-self watching the movie from the side of the young patient who was powerfully attracted to a woman, but frightened to make a commit-ment to her. When she discovered that he was not ready to take that step, she moved across the country and out of his life. That turn of events shook me. What if I moved so carefully that something like that happened to me?

We walked out of the theater. It was raining hard, I remember, and we ran to the car. I unlocked the car doors and we jumped in, already cold and wet through the outer layer of our clothes. But I hardly thought about that discomfort, because my chest felt so tight that I could hardly breathe. I said that the movie had really moved me, and then (as unexpected to me as it was to her) I burst into tears and said, "I want to spend the rest of my life with you." Until that moment, I hadn't uttered such a thought even in the privacy of my own mind although I had certainly wondered when and if it would get to the point of real commitment.

I sat there wondering whether I had made a terrible mistake in blurting out my feeling so suddenly, but Susan just held me in her arms. As we drove home a few minutes later, I realized that, completely without planning, I had taken a big step that I had not known, in my mind, how to take. Looking back on it, I felt happy and satisfied. I had gone with my heart, and the right thing had happened. I wondered where my life would end up, but I loving the country that it was entering.

As the date for the wedding approached, we maintained an intense schedule of work, which often kept us apart I suppose that if I had been doing it all myself, we would have been married in some matter-of-fact little ceremony. But Susan had a different dream, and the result was a very small, very beautiful ceremony. There were fifty people, mostly family, in a small candle-lit building at the edge of the San Francisco Bay. Everything was exquisite. At the end of the meal, in place of the traditional big wedding cake, each guest received a decorated, individual bite-sized "wedding cake."

We hadn't managed to carve out the time for a real honeymoon after the wedding, so we settled for a three-night trip to an inn set high on the cliffs above the Pacific at Big Sur. The night we arrived, a huge storm blew down from Alaska and enclosed our little cliff-side cabin in a roaring swirl of clouds and wind. Although our cabin was embedded in the soil and roofed with sod, it shuddered and rattled under the force of the storm, which was the biggest since a monster storm had washed out the highway to that part of the coast a year earlier. Throughout that stormy night, I woke from time to time and wondered if we were going to be blown off the cliff into the surf eight-hundred feet below. Each time I would think to myself, "If that happens, I'll die happy." And then I'd drift back to sleep.

I wonder as I write these words if some readers may think I am recommending that they stop worrying about whatever they are trying to decide in their lives and just Do It. "Follow your heart" sounds a little like "shut off your mind," but it is really quite different. All I am saying to shut off is that anxious search for the right answer—surely it's on file somewhere! The solution doesn't come from finding the right way to act but from finding your own way to go. To try to turn on your direction-finding mechanism at the eleventh hour is a sure way to miss the turn. You can't wait so long. Instead, you need to be tuned in way back at the time of the previous ending.

I suspect that is why, comparatively speaking, my own transition went relatively quickly. (Remarried within a year and a half? Gosh, that's fast!) But the transition didn't begin with Mondi's death. It began, and began with great intensity, when she and I started saying good-bye after her diagnosis two years earlier. Nor was it slowed down by all sorts of unfinished business. Our struggles over her affair with her psychotherapist were behind us; we had gone through that awful ending long before we discovered that she was ill. And it wasn't just that we had been at it for a long time. We had also gone over that ground repeatedly, for, as I began this book by saying we went through our ending over and over, as though saying good-bye, were an age-old ceremony that we were practicing.

The transition that included Mondi's death and my remarriage wasn't really such a brief one. And we weren't following any book of instructions ("The Way to Make a Successful Transition"). To have planned how to deal with that chapter of our lives according to some set of steps would have turned a meaningful experience into a mechanistic one in which we *managed* the situation instead of really *experiencing* it. Trying to be loving and supportive and conscious by means of technique robs your life and your relationship of the richness that comes from the build-up of unmediated experience, the whole whopping mess of joy and pain that living provides anyone who will stay open to it. One of the pitfalls of the *enlightened* outlook is that it gets selective. It opts for joy, it opts for sexual fulfillment, it opts for self-expression and openness and communication and sensitivity. In so doing, it cleans up the compost pile by sorting out all the weeds and the manure.

All of us wish we knew exactly what to do, but if such a book of *answers* actually existed, we would find ourselves faced with an even more serious problem. This book would make you and me unnecessary, because then the world would have no need for the unique person that each one of us is.[2] It is only in living out the unique way of your individual life and following the meandering journey that you have been on since you were born that you and I make the choices that are right for each of us. Without the necessity of living your way through the situations with which the world confronts you, *you'd have no life of your own.* For there isn't a bright, fresh-off-the-rack life hanging in the closet, waiting to be taken down and worn like a new coat.

That is why we are here: to go on our own personal meandering journeys and to be shaped by them. If that were unnecessary, we wouldn't be here, living the lives that we are living. How that all adds up to the great pattern of universal reality, I don't have a clue. But *that it does add up* is clear. Any particular acre of earth is inhabited by a particular group of creatures, each of which is busy living out his or her own particular journey. The interrelated paths of those journeys would make those whorls of multicolored wires in a telephone switching box look like an introduction-to-geometry diagram by comparison. What we call "reality" is nothing more, or less, than journeying going on at every level from the subatomic to the personal to the galactic.

• • •

A man's life of any worth is a continual
allegory. . . . a life like the scriptures, figurative.

John Keats

The external shape of my family slowly changed to incorporate Susan. Five years earlier, Mondi and I had begun taking the children and grandchildren on a biennial family trip to some warm place right after Christmas. The first time we went to Mexico, and the second time—already under the shadow of Mondi's cancer and scaled back because of her weakness—we settled for a hotel in Arizona. That time, my brother Dan and his daughter and her family joined us. Nineteen ninety-eight was family-trip time again, and this time we all went to a resort in Jamaica. It was Susan's first immersion in my family, and it gave everyone the chance to spend an extended period of time together. Susan paddled a kayak with her new granddaughter, Tyler, and took morning hikes with her new brother-in-law, Dan. She walked on the beach with her stepdaughters and took video-game instruction from her new grandsons. Every morning when we met for breakfast, she was a little more at home in the new group.

Five years before, while I was getting ready for the first family post-Christmas trip to Mexico, I had made some notes to capture what I saw in my present and my future. I had just turned sixty, and I thought that I ought to have some serious and deep Thoughts About Life. The other day I came across those notes and the agenda for the next five years that they contained. I don't know whether I really believed that I would follow it, but I wrote the items down in the hopes that putting possibilities into words would help me catch a glimpse of the life I'd encounter on the road ahead of me.

Mondi's cancer diagnosis was still a year away, so the biggest fact of my future was invisible to me. In my first item, I had said that I would publish a new book. That was hardly a brilliant guess, because I already had a contract for *JobShift* and was almost done with the manuscript. Next I had said that I would be semiretired. With all of the turmoil Mondi and I had been through in the previous few years, I was tired and more than a little depressed. I had thought that I could use a good rest, and at my age that readily translates into retirement. In fact, the kind of renewal that I have been describing in this chapter has brought me much more energy than any amount of rest would have. Although there were times during the past five years when I certainly considered calling it quits and although I have cut back in my travel schedule, I am still actively at work.

I had said that I would be taking stock and thinking about what kind of a legacy I was going to leave behind me, and that has been happening. This book is part of that impulse, for it represents a different kind of record of what I've been thinking—and one that will, I hope, provide readers with renewed courage to move forward through their own difficult times. Another part of that impulse had been a growing concern for those in our society who have a particularly hard time with the high rate of change and whose changes put their families into particularly difficult transitions. I had been thinking about how some of these ideas would play out in a societal context: What would our society do if it were to decide to offer its members assistance with transition, comparable to but different from the old rites of passage?

And how could I help younger people who feel very little support from their parents and who lack the circle of elders that once helped to shape the course of young lives? How could I support and involve myself in some of their projects to move the world in directions that I agree it must move. At this stage in my life, I don't have to play it safe any more and guard my reputation. I can afford to take a few chances. I am moving out of that time when I expressed my innate conservatism by being *responsible* and my innate radicalism by *knowing and showing my mastery* over whatever life threw at me.

At this point, my innate conservatism comes out more as a desire to connect the meanings of the past with the needs of the present— an effort to use whatever wisdom I have gained in losing what I thought that I couldn't stand to lose. And my innate radicalism comes out, not in mastering the challenges that I encounter but in the far quieter recognition that I not only can take risks, but that I want to.

When Odysseus had finally finished his long, hard homecoming voyage and had driven the would-be usurpers away from his home and his wife, he sat and tried to figure what to do next. It is said that he pondered then a prophecy that said he would gather what was left of his old crew and would move on to a strange and faraway land, so different from his own that there they could not distinguish a boat-oar from a wheat winnowing basket.

I don't know exactly what that meant to Odysseus, but to me it means moving on across a threshold separating the world I have known from a world that isn't even knowable in my old terms. I was thinking about that threshold the other night when I awoke from a dream, for the edge of sleep is another famous threshold. I had been dreaming that I was walking on my old college campus, showing around a male teen-ager and a young boy. I said some things to them about the excellence of the college faculty, the architecture of its eighteenth-century buildings, and the reputation of its graduates.

But then the scene changed. I had lost the two young people, and I was trying to find my way through and out of a building full of long corridors. Occasionally my wanderings would take me past a window through which I could see trees and people, but most of the time I was walking down hallways and through rooms. I was alone, and I wasn't getting anywhere. I knew that I would get out eventually, but it was taking a long, long time, and I was feeling increasingly frustrated. I wanted to return to the outer world of the campus.

In the image of my dream, I have been talking to people about important subjects in the outer world for a long time. My own inner "youths" had been impressed and had listened attentively. The talk that had impressed them had been useful, I think, but then unexpectedly my life took me back "inside." I spent a long while wandering my own inner corridors. By the end of the dream, I was ready to come out again and do something new. Odysseus was ready to move on to new challenges in a world that would be very different from the one in which he won his reputation, a world in which they didn't even recognize the boat-oar with which he had made the long voyage home.

I am ready. I've learned over this past quarter-century of working with transition that you can repress the future as well as the past. A hundred years ago, people began to study the unconscious, and they treated it as though it was made up of buried contents. Memories, wishes, fantasies—these were the "things" that the conscious mind could not deal with and that it hid away out of the light of awareness. That view represented the traditional world of nineteenth-century materialism, but it doesn't square with what we know of the universe today. Today, reality seems more like energy fields, vibrations and rhythms, or not-yet articulated patterns of movement. When I talk of repressing the future, it is such patterns and fields that I believe we do not let ourselves see.

But the future is there for each of us, in the form of a dimly sensed movement, a pattern that we can almost glimpse out the corner of our eye. To see and understand it, to grasp the opportunities that it foretells, we must always let go of our old way of seeing and of the understandings that carried us to this point in our lives. Ultimately we will come to the new understanding and the new reality, but that will not happen until we have wandered for what will seem like a frustratingly long time, looking for the door that will take us out into our new life.

The future also contains the past, for in the past there were foreshadowings of what would be, and the future will carry them as echoes. It is July again, as it was two years ago when I was just starting to notice the world again after Mondi's death in May. Walking my dog this morning, I came across two more black feathers. This must be molting season for crows, because I don't find these feathers at other times of the year. The sight of them took me back two years to the experience of seeing them as a message from Mondi. That thought returns this time, but only as an echo or an overtone. The past is still present, but as a remembered pattern under the surface of experience. Still a part of me. Forever a part of me.

•　　•　　•

In a Norwegian fairy tale, the hero came to a crossroads where there are three signs: "He who travels down this road will return unharmed"; "He who travels this path may or may not return"; and, "He who travels here will never return." Of course, he chose the third.

Laura Simms

It is night again, and we have just turned out the light. The interplay of light and dark is fascinating. Viewed statically, they are opposites and we usually favor light over dark. But viewed dynamically, their relation is more complex. In the morning, light is the deliverer, restoring what is *real* after a night of dreams and magnified imaginings. But at night it is the other way around. The *reality* of the day has flattened out into ordinariness. We are tired of the way it overwhelms us. In that state, the darkness is the release and the truthbringer. We wait to see what view of the other side of life's fabric, our dreams, will bring.

I snuggle up behind Susan as we lie there on our sides. I think to myself: The best thing we bought since we married was the new mattress for our bed. It's so comfortable. An image drifts past, and I almost grasp it. But it is gone. It might have been the answer, the key to the door that would take me out into the future, into the next stage in my journey. Maybe that's what the feathers were saying this morning. I drift. Susan stirs. I start to let go of the day and of its reality. Every night is a tiny transition. We get to practice letting go all the time. Another image drifts past. The darkness is that fertile inbetween place. It is the source of new form. I'm drifting into it. Goodnight. Goodnight. Good-bye. Letting go, then drifting. And then, out of nowhere. . .

an epilogue

To believe your own thought, to believe that what is true for you in your private heart is true for all men— that is genius. Speak your latent conviction, and it shall be the universal sense.

Ralph Waldo Emerson

There, done. This was the most difficult book to write of the ten that I've written. It forced me to go back over the ground of personal experience that was almost as hard to relive as it had been to go through the first time. But it was also hard because I kept worrying about how all the personal chapters would come across. All of my writing has been personal, but in most of it I've hidden that fact by clothing my own experience in generalities. *Transitions* (1980) grew out of the difficulties I had encountered in my own midlife career change; *JobShift* (1994) and *Creating You & Co.*(1997) simply laid out the rationale for the career as an independent worker that I myself had been following since the mid-seventies.

But in this book, I wanted to match my concepts against the real experience of an individual, for I believed that only in that way could I capture the deeper realities of being in transition. I can only say, as Thoreau did when he wrote about himself, I'd have used someone else if I had known their story as well as I knew my own.

When I started, I meant to keep my personal chapters and my conceptual chapters separate and to alternate them as a kind of counterpoint throughout the book. But the further I pushed into the subject, the harder that became. The "fishtailing" that I spoke of early in the book, moved me back and forth from the personal to the general more rapidly than I thought it would, and I found in the end that I had to follow the book where it wanted to go.

As I prepared to write this book, I read through journals that I kept in my forties and fifties. I came away from those visits to my past with two impressions that may at first seem to have little to do with each other. The first is how long it took me to learn how to say what I knew; and the second is how long I lived unhappily under the gray sky of feeling misunderstood. As I say, these two matters may seem to be unrelated, but in fact they are the halves of a single whole.

The first half is that although I had premonitions in my forties of how I might use writing to find (or even to create) my own reality, I didn't manage to do that more than episodically until I was sixty. More than that, I didn't recognize until I had started this book how much I could learn about myself from writing. I am a late bloomer, in art as in love. In both, it took me nearly a lifetime to learn to trust my heart.

The second half of my discovery dealt with how Mondi's view of me, both as a person and as a writer, led me to try to please and impress her. As the product of a family that constantly treated her badly and lied to her, she had a deep-seated suspicion of just about anything that people said to or did for her. And as the daughter of a very creative man who acted as though the buildings he designed were the real "children" that he had brought into the world, she could not help feeling that my writing was her rival for my heart.

These two things combined to encourage me to write with an eye on her approval and discouraged me from taking the creative risks that are necessary if one is to find one's own way in and through writing. On her side, those things made her suspicious of my writing and led her to consider it a kind of self-indulgence on my part. She viewed it that way especially when I was writing things that I had little prospect of being able to publish. "Why are you still working on that?" she would say, in a tone that implied that there were a dozen other things that I could have been doing that would have contributed more to our family's happiness and well-being.

Although she was also proud of the things that I did publish, her failure to understand the importance to me of writing *per se* made it difficult for me (as full of self-mistrust as I was) to understand and believe in it myself. I once wrote a novel, for example, which was turned down by more than twenty publishers. I always felt that that novel was the most valuable writing experience I had ever had, although when I said that, she found it hard to believe that I wasn't just making an excuse for those months when I didn't earn my share of the family expenses. When she heard that I was talking with the psychotherapist I was seeing at that same time about writing instead of my personal difficulties, she viewed it as my avoidance of the issues that I ought to be working on. And when, only a couple of years before she died, she came across a box of folders full of notes I had kept from my unfinished writing projects through the years, she just shook her head in disbelief.

I used to resent these attitudes and behaviors, and for years that resentment bubbled up in all sorts of covert and even unconscious ways. She said that I was hostile and that I used a travel-laden and work-centered life to keep my distance from her. And she was right. But what neither she nor I could see was not how much I needed to change, but how important it was to my development that she withheld her approval as she did. Since it kept me from ever really believing that I could win that approval, it forced me to understand and appreciate the role of writing in my life myself, on my own terms. It held me back from a too-easy identification of myself as a writer and meant that I had to work hard for that identity—not simply by laboring at writing and by succeeding in publishing the results, but also by working hard to overcome my self-doubts. The fact that I got little help from her in overcoming them meant that writing became not only a vehicle for self-discovery but for self-affirmation as well.

Her lack of support combined with the success I had had with more practical writing about organizational change kept me away from individual and personal topics for a long time. When I did return, I rediscovered how deeply the act of writing could move me. I had forgotten what it was like to be so seized by the excitement of ideas taking shape in my mind that I sat jotting notes at stoplights while cars behind me revved their engines and honked. I had forgotten how excited I could be to find out what was just around the bend of whatever I was writing. What a pleasure it was to rediscover the thrill of seeing the ground appear before my eyes just as I was about to take my next step.

More than anything, writing this book has enabled me to remember what an important thread of continuity writing has been in my life. At each of my important turning points, I had used writing to illuminate my path. And here it is again, in the form of this book itself, linking who I was before Mondi's death to who I am now at this point of renewal and redirection in my life. It is the light that I carry to shine down the dark corridor of my own aging and to make visible the joys of getting older. It helps me to explain and show how you can always begin again, as long as you are on your own path. Framing it all is the fact that it is writing that enables me to describe in general and to record in particular what happens when your life plunges you into transition.

In the end, transition is my gateway into the subject that I have wanted to write about. That subject is life itself and the way that it falls naturally into the meandering shape of the journey. Many people, who purport to advise us on the art of living, talk about doing things in a linear, rational, efficient way. My own view is that such efforts are like a project to improve a country landscape by cutting all the trees and planting a nice smooth lawn.

Life is not, after all, a football contest against an opponent where you are trying to gain yardage in a linear movement toward some imaginary goal line. You do not score by progressing across the whole field. Life is more like baseball, where the motion is not the push-pull of opposing forces under a fixed time limit. In baseball you go around the bases, and you score by completing a circle. "Time" is not clock-time, but is dictated by what happens in the game itself on the field.

The motion of life is circular too. Unlike linear and mechanical motion, we start and end at the same point, although when we have gone around the bases we are credited with a run. It isn't force against counterforce or push against resistance, for circles are shaped by other forces. The earth sails onward like a rock whirled out of a sling, but the sun draws it sideways. It doesn't oppose it. There is just an attraction from another dimension, not the old push-pull but a drawing-toward that bends the path around until it arcs back on itself—and we find ourselves home again.

But not home again too. As the man said, you can't go home again, even though (as the planets remind us) you are always trying to come full circle. But you don't, not quite, because just before the loop can be completed, you find yourself trying to flow uphill, against gravity, and so you head seaward again in another looping attempt at a circle, which similarly fails to complete itself. Life meanders in this way. Art gives us all kinds of images of this living path that goes where it is going in a series of incomplete circles. There is the serpent of knowledge in the garden, the twisting pathway through the maze, the caduceus, or staff, of Mercury, and there are the twisting branches of the tree of life. Living is a meandering pathway across the void.

Just what causes the timing of these turnings is beyond our knowing. We have about as much of a grasp of their timing as an intestinal bacterium has of the human meal-times that cause the ebb and flow of the nutriment that sustains it. All we know is that periodically, some situation or event deflects us from the path that we thought we were on and, in so doing, ends the life-chapter we were in. In order to continue our journey, we are forced to let go of the way we got that far. Having let go, we find ourselves in the wilderness for a time, and not until we have lived out that time can we come back around to a new beginning.

The Greeks told the story of life's journey of self-renewal this way:[1]

Demeter was the goddess of growing things, particularly of grain. We still recall her every time we speak of *cereal*, for that food was named after what she was called by the Romans, *Ceres*. The Greek story tells of a time before time, when things grew constantly in a seasonless world. One day Demeter's daughter, Persephone, was picking flowers in a meadow, when Hades, the god of the Underworld, saw and fell in love with her. Being as untroubled by mortal niceties as the gods were, Hades simply rose up out of the earth and took her down to his dark kingdom as his bride.

Back upstairs, Persephone's mother looked everywhere for her daughter. In her grief, Demeter neglected to watch over the growing grain, and it turned from green to gold and then to a dry brown. The air grew colder, the days shorter. Frightened by the strange changes, people rushed about to gather what grain they could, as the incomprehensible first winter came on.

Somehow word of what had actually happened to Persephone finally reached Demeter, and she went to the land of the gods, atop Mt. Olympus, to ask Zeus, her father and the greatest of the gods, to tell Hades to release his granddaughter at once. In the scattered realms and divided powers of the gods, things were not that simple, however. Hades was Zeus's brother and was nearly his equal. And Hades meant to have his own way. But Zeus did intercede, and finally Hades agreed to give up his youthful queen.

Everything seemed to be settled, and people expected the eternal summer to return again. Suddenly, however, an unexpected problem arose. An obscure little Underworld gardener announced that he had seen Persephone eat some pomegranate seeds, and the whole plan to get her back collapsed. For whoever eats anything in the land of death can no longer return as before to the land of the living. Persephone was no longer immortal, for now death was lying inside her, like a seed waiting for sprouting-time.

The arrangements to deal with this turn of events took too long to tell, but at last it was agreed that Persephone would spend nine months above ground and three months of each year in the Underworld. When she was down there with Hades, everything above ground would grow dark and cold. The grain would stop growing and would be gathered and stored in order to get through this strange new season, winter. When she left the Underworld at the end of the dark season, spring would come again, grain would sprout and a new phase of growth would begin over again.

That is how the Greeks explained the living rhythm of fullness and loss that we call the seasons. But the story does more than that, for it also speaks in ways that reach deeper than any logic, of life's deep need to renew itself and to die before it can experience life anew. We have to go downward before we can rise, to end the old before we can begin over again.

From the point of view of the story's actors, the final arrangement was a compromise. But from the story's point of view, the resulting cycle of living and dying was the whole point. The eating of the pomegranate seeds was much more than a sad mistake, and the outcome was far more than an unhappy compromise. For the ending and the lower part of the cycle that it initiates is as necessary as is the reemergence from the darkness when the new beginning occurs. Everywhere in nature, birth is an expulsion, the loss of the safe, known world that has been our home.

And so it is with each crossing that we make during the lifetime, and so it will be at the end of our lives, when our next step begins with the loss of another safe, known world.

. . . which brings me back to where I was when my own life was swallowed up in the darkness of loss, and I found myself in transition.

notes

Chapter One

1. From a letter written to William Smith, January 9, 1795.

2. Throughout this book, "ending" and "loss" and "letting go" will be used more or less interchangeably, for they represent different facets of the same experience. "Ending" will be how I refer to the break between you and whatever you have been identifying with. "Losing" is what I'll call it when I am emphasizing the experience of having to make that ending. And "letting go" is what I'll call it when I am talking about what you have to do to deal with the ending and the loss.

3. An English translation of the book by Monika B. Vizedom and Gabrielle L. Chaffee was published in paperback by the University of Chicago Press in 1960.

4. Cutchogue (NY, Buccaneer Books, 1976), p. 131.

5. We go through changes, without going through transition, all the time. In such cases we come out of the experience the same person as we went in. But when we are "ripe" for transition, even a relatively small change can lead to a transformative transition.

6. *What Is Art?* trans. V. Tchertkoff (1898).

Chapter Two

1. She is referring to a passage in Etty Hillesum, *An Interrupted Life: The Diaries of Etty Hillesum, 1941–1943*, (1983).

2. Meredith Willson, "Goodnight, My Someone," *The Music Man,* (Burbank, CA: Warner Bros. Records, 1962).

Chapter Three

1. See Mircea Eliade, *The Sacred and the Profane,* trans. Willard Trask (New York: Harcourt, Brace, Jovanovich, 1959).

2. Ralph Waldo Emerson, "Nature," *The Complete Works of Ralph Waldo Emerson* (Boston, 1903–4), Vol. I, p. 4.

Chapter Four

1. "Grieving" comes from an ancient root-word meaning "heavy" and refers to the feeling that accompanies a loss. "Mourning," on the other hand, comes from a root-word referring to "remembering." The latter therefore deals more with the way that the mind works on the broken connection, while the former deals more with the sadness and depression that is the result of the break.

Chapter Five

1. See Tu Wei-Ming, "The Confucian Perception of Adulthood," *Daedalus* [Issue on Adulthood] (Spring 1976): 109–23; the quote is taken from p. 117.

2. For examples of ritual disenchantment, see Sam D. Gill, "Disenchantment," in *Parabola* (Summer, 1976), pp. 6–13.

3. Christopher Frye, *A Yard of Sun* (1970), Act II.

4. Homer, *The Odyssey,* trans. Albert Cook (New York: W. W. Norton, 1967), XII, ll. 226–30. For an extended discussion of the epic from this point of view, see my earlier book, *Transitions: Making Sense of Life's Changes* (New York: Perseus Books, 1980), pp. 47–52.

5. This alternating current, which characterizes our breathing, is built in to the original patterns of spiritual thought. When it says in the Book of Exodus that "in six days God made heaven and earth, and on the seventh day God rested and was refreshed," the original Hebrew literally says that on the seventh day God "exhaled." See Wayne Muller, *Sabbath: Restoring the Sacred Rhythm of Rest* (New York: Bantam Books, 1999), p. 36.

6. In *Under the Tuscan Sun* (New York: Broadway Books, 1996), p. 124. Italics added.

7. *The Viking Book of Aphorisms*, selected by W. H. Auden and Louis Kronenberger (New York: Dorset Books, 1962), p. 157.

Chapter Six

1. Alvin Toffler, *Future Shock* (New York: Bantam Books, 1990), p. 255.

Chapter Seven

1. I use this term in the sense that Carl Jung used it to refer to inherent psychic patterns that are animated by some symbol: the mother-figure as the symbol of life's natural generativity, the return of life in the spring as an image of rebirth after death, the wise old person as an image of the wisdom that comes from living itself, and the bird as an image of the spirit. But, as Jung pointed out, traditional portrayals of archetypal patterns often lose their power to stir us. "Eternal truth needs a human language that alters with the spirit of the times," he wrote in *The Psychology of the Transference* (1946). "The primordial images undergo ceaseless transformation and yet ever remain the same, but only in a new form can they be understood anew. Always they require a new interpretation if, as each formulation becomes obsolete, they are not to lose their [power]. . . " Then he adds provocatively, "Where are the answers to the spiritual needs and troubles of [our] new epoch? And where is the knowledge to deal with the psychological problems raised by the development of modern consciousness?" Quoted in *Psychological Reflections*, p. 45.

2. P. M. Allen, "The Evolutionary Paradigm of Dissipative Structures," in E. Jantsch, ed., (Denver: Westview Press, 1981), p. 27, quoted in Stickland, p. 132.

3. *Ibid., p. 70.*

Chapter Eight

1. I printed the book before finding that Levinson had chosen a similar title for his *Seasons of A Man's Life.* The publication of my book was funded by a loan from a mentor and good friend, Jim Ingebretsen.

Chapter Nine

1. This translation of the poetry that was part of the scroll was posted by the museum next to the scroll itself.

2. Keats used and explained the term in a letter he wrote to G. and T. Keats, December 21, 1817.

3. *The Experience of Nothingness* (New York: Harper & Row, 1970), p. 70.

4. Two books that contain the examples that follow, as well as many more, are John A. B. McLeish, *The Ulyssean Adult: Creativity in the Middle and Later Years* (Toronto: McGraw-Hill-Ryerson, 1976) and Alex Comfort, *A Good Age* (New York: Crown, 1976).

5. I first heard this distinction between "decision" and "choice" from the coauthor of *The Art of Japanese Management,* Anthony Athos, although I don't think that I understood it at the time—or until I found myself facing and making this important choice.

6. Karlfried Graf von Durckheim, *The Japanese Cult of Tranquility* (New York: Samuel Weiser, 1974), pp. 46–47.

Chapter Ten

1. John Gardner and Francesca Gardner Reese, eds., *Quotations of Wit and Wisdom* (NY: W.W. Norton, 1975), p. 42.

2. For more about how to manage organizational transition, see *Managing Transition* (Cambridge, MA: Perseus Books, 1991).

3. *Genesis* 32:11.

4. *Letters to a Young Poet,* p. 92.

5. Chapter XXV.

6. Matthew 5:48.

7. *The Illustrated Bible Dictionary,* 3 vols., [Various editors], (Wheaton, Ill.: Tyndale House Publishers, 1980), Vol. 3, p. 1190. In its most fundamental sense, *sin* refers to a break or incompleteness in the natural pattern of development rather than a dent in the shiny fender of life. In secular Greek, the word here translated "perfect" meant also "adult, full grown, as opposed to immature and infantile." *Ibid.*

Chapter Eleven

1. James Geick, *Chaos: Making a New Science* (NY: Viking, 1987), p. 67.

2. This way of thinking about why each of us is necessary was first suggested to me years ago by James Bugental, the existential psychologist who replaced Abraham Maslow in my Summer Workshop for College Teachers in 1970.

An Epilogue

1. Paraphrased from Robert Graves, *The Greek Myths* (Baltimore, Md: Penguin Books, 1955), Vol. I, pp. 89–96.